# MAKING MONEY *for* TEENS

The Teenagers Guide to Personal Finance:
How to Save, Invest, Build Your Wealth
and Become Richer than Your Parents

PHOENIX READ

© **Copyright 2021 – All rights reserved**

The content contained within this book may not be reproduced, duplicated, or transmitted without direct written permission from the author or the publisher.

Under no circumstances will any blame or legal responsibility be held against the publisher, or author, for any damages, reparation, or monetary loss due to the information contained within this book, either directly or indirectly.

**Legal Notice:**

This book is copyright protected. It is only for personal use. You cannot amend, distribute, sell, use, quote, or paraphrase any part, or the content within this book, without the consent of the author or publisher.

**Disclaimer Notice:**

Please note the information contained within this document is for educational and entertainment purposes only. All effort has been executed to present accurate, up-to-date, reliable, complete information. No warranties of any kind are declared or implied. Readers acknowledge that the author is not engaged in the rendering of legal, financial, medical, or professional advice. The content within this book has been derived from various sources. Please consult a licensed professional before attempting any techniques outlined in this book.

By reading this document, the reader agrees that under no circumstances is the author responsible for any losses, direct or indirect, that are incurred due to the use of the information contained within this document, including, but not limited to, errors, omissions, or inaccuracies.

# Table of Contents

**Introduction** ......................................................... 1

**Chapter 1: Money Responds to Your Attitude and Mindset**................................................... 9

   Common Money Mistakes Teenagers Make ........... 12

   Know the Difference Between What You Need and What You Want......................................... 23

   Your Financial Life is Important, Don't Leave it to Chance ................................. 26

   How Teens Waste Money on Useless Items............ 27

**Chapter 2: Money Basics – Making, Saving and Spending Money**..................................... 39

   Start Making Money Now ....................................... 40

   Tips to Help You on the Job .................................. 66

**Chapter 3: Savings & Banking – Strategies for Growing Your Wealth** ............................ 69

   Reasons Why You Need to Start Saving Today....... 70

      *You Would be Learning Financial Literacy* ............ 71

      *It's Your Path to Independence and Self-reliance* ... 71

 *Helps You Spend Wisely* ............................................. *72*
 *Help Prepare You for Access to Financial Products* *73*
 *You Can Achieve Your Financial Goals* ................... *73*
 *Tips to Improve Your Saving Culture* ....................... *74*
Teens Guide to Banking & Financial Products ...... 77
 *Deposit* ................................................................... *78*
 *Withdrawal* ............................................................ *79*
 *Types of Bank Accounts* ......................................... *79*
 *Banking Fees* ......................................................... *82*
 *How You Spend Your Money* ................................... *83*

## Chapter 4: Budgeting Basics – The Real Secret to Managing Your Wealth ............................. 87

 Understand Your Earnings ................................... 88
 Break it Down ....................................................... 88
 Select a Budgeting Strategy ................................. 90
 Save Now and Spend Later ................................... 91
 Set a Goal-Oriented Budget .................................. 92
 Spending Adjustment ............................................ 92
 Adjust Your Budget ............................................... 93
 Learn from Your Mistakes .................................... 93
 Earn More with Side Gigs .................................... 94
 Spend Moderately ................................................. 94
 Avoid Peer Pressure ............................................. 95
 Ask for Help ........................................................... 95
 Balance Your Budget ............................................ 96
 Please, Have Fun .................................................. 96

Negative Implications of not Having a Budget ........ 97
Debts Will Kill Your Dreams of Becoming Rich .... 100
    *Your Freedom Depends on Your Level of Debt* ...... *101*
    *Back Off from Credit Card Debts* .......................... *102*
    *Invest in Your Retirement Today* ......................... *102*
    *Choose Your School Wisely* .................................. *102*
    *Little Expenses Lead to Big Problems* ................... *103*

## Chapter 5: Investment – Growing and Multiplying Your Wealth ............................ **105**

When Can You Start Investing? ............................ 106
How to Invest as a Teen ....................................... 109
    *Investment in Individual Stocks* ............................ *109*
    *Investment in Mutual Funds* ................................ *111*
    *Investment in Index Fund ETFs* ........................... *111*
    *Let's Talk About Micro Investing Apps* .................. *113*
How to Start Investing Today ............................... 114
What's All the Hype About Cryptocurrency? ........ 116
What exactly is a cryptocurrency? ....................... 117
Here's How Cryptocurrencies Work ..................... 117
What is the value of cryptocurrency? ................... 119
    *Bitcoin* .................................................................. *119*
    *Ethereum* .............................................................. *120*
    *NFTs* ..................................................................... *120*
    *Chainlink* .............................................................. *121*
How Teens Can Invest in Cryptocurrency ............ 122
    *Greyscale* .............................................................. *122*

*Transfer*.................................................................... *123*
*Peer to peer exchanges* ......................................... *124*
The Story of the Tampa Teen Who Made
Thousands from Cryptocurrency..................... 125

**Conclusion** ...................................................... **127**

**A Plea From the Author** ................................. **133**

**References**....................................................... **135**

# Introduction

Do you know any teenager out there making tons of money, and you wish it were you? You see them on TV and follow them on social media even when you don't expect them to follow back. Some of these teenagers are about your age or even younger. Maybe you have even thought of how you can be like them, but you can't figure it out yet.

You have talked with your friends about it, but they thought you were joking. Even after talking with your parents, they seem not to know how to help bring out the millionaire in you. They probably want you to focus on college to avoid distractions.

First, I need you to know you're not crazy for wanting to make lots of money. Those young people you desire to be like are not aliens; they are primarily regular teenagers or younger. Some of them didn't even get any form of support from their parents, they just had the right attitude and mindset, and the rest, as they say, is history.

Let me start by telling you the story of Christian Owen, a teenager like you, and what he did to start making good money. I'm talking about real money and hundreds of thousands of it. Then I will go into what you need to do to start making your fantasies a reality; you don't have to wait until you finish college or when you're 30-years-old.

## The Story of Christian Owens

Christian Owens probably became famous when he launched his first company, Mac Bundle, in 2008. He was only 14-years-old at that time, and the company was valued at £700,000 ($947,646). What many did not know was that Christian had been using a computer since he was a child. At age seven, he had started teaching himself web designing, and by age 10, he got a Mac as a gift.

The teenager noticed how expensive some of the apps on Mac were and realized some organizations would be spending up to $540 on apps they needed to carry out their operation. He then negotiated with several manufacturers and distributors to offer a bundle package of applications for Mac OS X for a lesser amount. The arrangement put the price of bundled apps at $100 instead of $540. The plan was an instant hit, and the rest is history.

The teenager who has vowed not to stop until he gets to $100,000,000 went on to launch a second company called "Branchr." This second company was an instant hit on the internet, and he raked in more than

$676,975 in its first year. Branchr is a pay-per-click advertising platform where buyers of advertisement content buy what the sellers have to offer.

Even though he was not of betting age, he had betting site clients such as William Hills. Branchr's services were also used by social networking sites such as Myspace when it first launched. And to think, he only worked on Branchr after school and over the weekends.

The young lad who lived with his parents' company secretary and a factory worker father said he was inspired by the incredible feats achieved by Steve Jobs. He said all he wanted to do was create something simple that would change the way advertising worked.

When asked about the secrets of his success. He said there was no magic formula to his success, but it takes hard work, determination, and the drive to succeed to create something great. He further explained that he believes everyone has a business sense, and all that is required to become great is some experience and determination.

In his words, *"Mac Box Bundle was already becoming a success, but I really wanted to push myself and do something different, so I came up with the idea of Branchr."* *"My aim is to become a leading name in the world of internet and mobile advertising and push myself right to the top of the game."* Extracted from Daily Mail August 13, 2010.

Branchr is a platform where website owners sell advertising content, and business owners go there to buy it. The company sells more than 300 million adverts to more than 11,000 websites monthly and has since bought over another smaller company, Atomplan, responsible for providing business software.

Christian has since launched a third company called Paddle.com.

Did you notice that this Christian was not born with a silver spoon? No, he was not; instead, he was a regular boy in the neighborhood, only he was not regular. He had a different mindset and attitude. He was determined to be great. He desired to live his dream, and he pursued it until his fantasies started becoming real.

The teenager made the most of his age and the time he had in his hands by solving problems, and the money came in eventually. He made his first million as a teenager. You can do the same and even better, and I will show you how it is possible.

Allow me to hold your hands as we go through the chapters to unravel the secrets of your first million dollars as a teenager.

## Still to Come

Having interacted with young people across several countries for more than ten years, I have had to listen to tens and hundreds of teens and pre-teens talk about their struggles. It's clear that every teenager wants to make their own money, but some lack the knowledge and drive to make it happen.

Below are some of the challenges I have noticed with young people and the limitations they are dealing with preventing them from breaking into the "millionaires teen club."

- They are tired of sourcing the internet for helpful information on making legitimate money virtually or physically.
- The little information available is filled with financial jargon and bogus phrases that leave them more confused than ever before.
- Although they are young, they want to start making their own money and be financially independent.
- They believe the stock market is too risky, and it's not their "thing" for now.
- They are curious about cryptocurrency and will love the opportunity to be guided correctly.

## What this book will do for you

This book is a "tell it all." With this book, I intend to hold your hand while navigating through some of these issues that have seemed impossible or difficult for you before now. Here are some of the things you will learn in this book.

- **I will share several secrets of your favorite teenager millionaires.** Who they were before hitting big and what they did to make it big. Some of these stories will shock you, trust me.

- **You will learn how to make money, save money and how to spend it.** The principles you have been missing all this while and how they can transform you from an average teenager to the envy of your friends and family.

- I have been able to identify those critical personal finance terms that have proved difficult to you; **I will show you fun ways to do them and have better results.**

- Some habits will prevent you from making it big financially, but you didn't know them before now. I will expose them all in this book.

- I will show you fun ways of working with a budget and the importance of having a record of all your transactions.

- I know you probably don't know much about debts and how they can stand in the way of you becoming wealthy. **I will guide you on how to manage that too.**

- **This book will guide you on how to multiply your money through investments.**

  You will also learn how to start making money from the stock market.

- Suppose you're struggling with how to be financially responsible. I will guide you through it because I know this can make or mar your financial success.

## Who is Phoenix Read?

Phoenix Read, Ph.D., is an author and researcher dedicated to debunking the secret of lifetime income maximization. He devotes his time to helping individuals, families, couples, and young people better manage and plan their wealth in this dynamic, complex, and stressful new era.

Read has been working with pre-teens and teenagers worldwide for more than a decade and understands their desires and pains. He has learned how to think like them to better proffer the right solutions for these young people.

As you read from one chapter to the other, you will feel his authority and devotion to wealth creation and management, especially young people. With a doctorate in social science, Phoenix Read has shown his dedication to social and financial issues in this book.

He has written this book to guide young people on making money and ultimately becoming financially responsible.

Phoenix Read is currently based in Ottawa, Canada.

*Chapter 1*

# Money Responds to Your Attitude and Mindset

I had tried hard to remember my activities when I was thirteen, but nothing remarkable came to mind. So, I'm throwing the question to you. If you are under thirteen, what are you doing with your time? For those of you above thirteen, what did you do when you were at that age?

Let me guess; you were probably like me, who was a good teenager, went to school, came back and did his homework, then went out to play with other teens in the neighborhood. As long as I was out of trouble, my parents and I were cool. However, I did not make money, neither did I take out a loan of $8,000 to start my own business. That was precisely what Emil Motycka did when he was thirteen and in his eighth grade. He took a loan of $8,000 from the bank to purchase a commercial lawn mower and set up his company, Motycka Enterprises.

Emil was not born with a silver spoon. He was just like any regular young lad like you and me; the only difference is he decided to do something different. The lad had always been obsessed with making money for himself since he was much younger. When he was in his first grade, he picked stray golf balls from a nearby course, cleaned them up, and resold them for a dollar each. He did this and many little businesses for some time. So, his parents were not surprised when he informed them that he wanted to start a business.

The question then is, why mowing, and where did the idea come from?

One time, his uncle asked him to mow his lawn and offered him $10. He completed the task nicely and thought he could offer the neighbors the same service at the same rate; that was how he became famous for lawn mowing. At age thirteen, Emil founded his lawn mowing company earning him his first one million dollars in his final year in high school.

From then on, the teenager had not looked back. He has been featured in Entrepreneur.com and recognized by Inc Magazine and has had the privilege of visiting the White House, where he was honored for his business successes.

Emil Motycka did not have any business experience when he started selling golf balls for one dollar each. The only thing in his head back then was that he wanted to make money. Even when his uncle offered him $10 to mow his lawn, the young lad was still in high school, but he offered value in exchange for money.

He was a quick thinker and figured he could make more money if he offered his uncle's neighbors the same service at the same rate. You could tell he always wanted to do something for himself. Let's face it, lawn mowing was not particularly a cool idea back then and even today, but he found a way to make money from it.

Motycka Enterprises today offers all types of gardening and light installation services with nearly a hundred staff.

Christian Owen made his first million while he was a teenager by bundling apps. Now you are reading about Emil Motycka, who made his first million before he finished high school mowing lawns. That tells you money can be made anywhere, even from unlikely sources. It's all about the mindset.

These young people and many more out there are proof that to make money. It's not about the education, or the skills, not even the money but the mindset and attitude.

## Common Money Mistakes Teenagers Make

In my many years of working with teenagers, I noticed that many teenagers don't know that money matters. They don't know why they must make their own money; some don't even think it's possible. Another group is just content with whatever their parents can afford instead of deliberately changing their situation.

So, as teenagers, you need to identify these common money mistakes and correct some attitudes and mindsets generally. Your mindset and attitude about making money will go a long way to determine how you approach the matter. A wrong mindset could mean you are just sitting and watching other young people make all the money while watching them on TV and following them on social media.

Below are some common mistakes I have identified, and I want you to avoid making the same.

## It's Too Early to Start Thinking About Money

Top on the list of these mistakes teenagers make is telling themselves that it's way too early for them to start making money. This is a common assumption among teenagers who have parents and guardians who can care for their needs.

It would help if you corrected this mindset and attitude that makes you feel it's too early to bother making money. Frankly speaking, it's never too early. The money habits and management that you develop now will get better as you grow older, shaping your future along the line.

EvanTube is a YouTube channel started by Evan when he was just eight years old. Today, he is making well over $1.3 million every year from this channel and has more than 7 million subscribers to his channels. I guess this is that part where you ask, what are his videos about?

If you have never heard of him before now, I bet you will not believe his videos are all about reviewing toys and other play items for children of his age. Companies now send their toys to Evan to have them reviewed before they get to the open market. What he feels and says about their toys matters a lot to them, and they are paying good money for it.

So, if you still think you're too young to start making money, please, think again.

## My Pocket Money is too Little to Save Anything

If you have been telling yourself this line, I would like to announce to you that you're WRONG!

Remember, we are dealing with mindset and attitude. So, if you tell yourself it's not possible, then indeed, it will appear impossible. However, if you have a drop of faith and you're willing to give it a shot, then you will be able to save something, no matter the size of your allowances.

This book will teach you how to save something from your allowances, no matter how little you are getting from your parents and guardians.

## I'm too Young to Earn Money

Here's another common mistake that prevents teenagers from making good money. Many young people believe they are too young to make money. They are just not bothered about earning money, mainly because their parents still cover their needs. There's another set of teens who do not even know what they can do to earn money, so they conclude they will take care of all that when they become adults.

It would help if you were willing to change this attitude and start learning ways to earn money for yourself. We will be sharing several choices you can choose from on how to start earning money.

## Dropping Out of School

I find this mistake interesting. Many teenagers I have worked with over the years who managed to start their businesses feel the need to drop out of school. Some believe that they need more time to build their business, while others want to drop out because it sounds like a cool thing to do.

Studies have shown that people who went through school make more money than those who drop out of high school. The reason for this is simple; often, to get a high-paying job, you will need a college degree. Research further discovered that people with masters' degrees earn $17,000 more than people with regular undergrad degrees. $17,000? Now that's a lot of difference. People with Bachelor's degrees also make more money than those without.

So, think about it again before you drop out of college. Do not end up making a mistake that will be difficult to correct as you grow up. If you have a business running and doing well, create time for both schooling and business. The higher your education qualification, the more likely you will make better decisions.

## I'm too Young to Bother About Business

Almost everywhere I went in my many travels over the years, the statement, "I'm too young to start a business," was common among teens. It makes me wonder where the idea came from. It's a very wrong and unacceptable mindset. Some of the names you are familiar with today, like Bill Gates, Mark Cuban, and Michael Dell, started running their businesses when they were teenagers.

Stop making statements like "business is not for everyone." That short statement is loaded with excuses and a poor attitudinal approach to entrepreneurship. Rather than make excuses, why not go out there and give it a shot. Your teenage years or earlier is the best time to know if you are cut out for business or not.

If you're a teenager, here are some of the reasons why now is the best time to start a business;

- At this age, your responsibilities are not as much as you will have in a few years to come.

- If you fail in business, you can try again, and if it doesn't work at all, you can get a job. Age is on your side.

- At this age, you have the rare opportunity of investing more free time into building your business. Time is your friend.

- Starting early also means you can start planning your retirement savings earlier.

## Becoming More Extravagant

There was a time when the word "extravagance" was only associated with the rich, but it is no longer the case. Instagram, YouTube, TikTok, and Snapchat keep pushing the button on consumerism. They make you believe people are living perfect lives. Companies like Microsoft, Apple, and others are paying influencers millions of dollars and spending a whole lot more on advertisements targeted at teens who like to buy more of their products.

All of these are making teenagers and millennials become more consumers than ever before. Young people will do anything to get the latest Microsoft Surface, iPhone, and other devices even when they serve the same purpose as those they previously owned. These desires have led to increasing levels of debt among young people. I will show you how a great budget can prevent you from falling into debt.

**Warning**: Stay away from debt as much as possible.

Unfortunately, teenagers who get into debt find it difficult to make it big in life. The reason is that you will be spending a considerable portion of your income from business or work servicing your debts. Gradually, you will become a slave to your debtors because they control your pockets. It gets even worse if you don't change your consumer attitude.

Some well-known gadgets and habits throw teenagers into gradual debts until it grows into something uncontrollable.

- Regularly hanging out at fancy restaurants.
- Thirst and acquisition of luxury designer brands like Prada, Gucci, Tommy Hilfiger, and the likes
- The subscription on boxes like Dollar Shave Club and BirchBox
- The quest to get the latest iPhones and Apple Watch
- Spending endless time gaming online
- Gambling away your income.

## Not Planning for Retirement

The majority of teenagers I interact with give me that "don't be ridiculous look" whenever this topic is brought up. That's because they have associated retirement with being old, and they think they still have a long time to get to that point. Teenagers don't want to think or talk about retirement; they believe it is still far off. Well, that is a big mistake that can hurt you in a few years to come.

The best time to start preparing for your retirement is when you are under 20. Don't let your friends tell you it's too early or that you have a whole life ahead of you. Check this out, do you know that if you are between 15 and 19 years old and you put away $25 every month, you will have more than $11,000 when you turn 60?

If you delayed and started saving the same $25 when you get to 30 because you felt you could not be bothered before now, you will only have about $7,000 or less. Imagine having to live on that for 15 years after you retire.

So, change your attitude and mindset about retirement and start now. Often, it's not about the amount but the commitment. We will be talking a little more about retirement in the book later.

## Failure to learn New Skills

As a teenager, you need to know that time is the best thing going for you. It's not even money but time. With that time in your hands, you can do a lot with it. However, I have seen many of you make the mistake of not being interested in learning anything new. You want to be done with school and be free.

That may sound true, but it is a mistake. Now is the best time to learn new skills, and you can learn them at your own pace. You are not under any form of pressure like your schoolwork, but it is imperative because you never know how it will help you in the future.

Remember the story of Christian Owen? He taught himself web designing before he was a teenager. He had all the time to test and practice the skill until he became an expert at it and set up a business that changed his life. Web designing was not on his school curriculum, but he learned it on his own online.

Today, there are loads of platforms where you can learn new skills, and they include;

- EDX
- Skillshare
- Udacity
- iversity
- Khan university
- Coursera

You never know what will change your financial status until you try it out. Start today by changing your mindset and attitude and start avoiding these common mistakes teenagers make.

## Know the Difference Between What You Need and What You Want

There's a common mistake adults make about teenagers; they often wonder what they need so much money for or why they need money at all.

One thing about teenagers and money is that teenagers love to have money and spend it—the same way adults love to have money to spend. There's no age discrimination when it comes to money. Before you ask a teenager what they need money for, make sure you have a pen and paper close by because the list is usually endless.

As teens, having money gives you a good feeling because you have loads of stuff you want to do with your money. At the same time, your whole day could go wrong with your mood messed up because you don't have the money you need to buy the things you desire.

As a young lad, I grew up to know the value of money beyond using it to get my immediate cravings. Interestingly, no one taught me this principle, not my parents, not even my teachers. Still, as important as this matter is, it is one of the least talked about at home and in schools. That has led to several young people making mistakes because they thought they had it all figured out, only to face the reality of life. For example, can you tell the difference between your needs and your wants?

Teenagers are constantly under pressure to live up to their peers. For example, your friends are getting the latest iPhones, buying and wearing designer clothes from top to bottom. Their hairstyles are the latest, shoes and bags are on point, and they pay their bills. Indeed, you will desire to live like and feel among. However, if you don't know the difference between what you need and what you want, you may end up wasting money on things you don't need. You might even be under unnecessary pressure.

What really is a **need** and a **want**?

A need is a requirement, something you can't do without, while a want is a desire, a wish. You can do without want, but you can't do without a requirement. Let's make it more straightforward. When you are hungry, you need food, right? What do you do? You enter a restaurant and order food; then, after a while, you ask the waiter for some fancy drink to support the food you ordered.

That food was a need because you required it to kill the hunger, but you see that fancy drink. It was a want, a desire, and you could do without it. If you didn't have the drink, you would still have been fine.

Let's use a more familiar teenage example. A need is that sweatshirt you need but don't have, and the weather is getting colder by the day. A want is that designer jacket a couple of friends in school have and makes them look classy and different in school. You would love to have one too, even though you have a jacket that can serve the same purpose but you desire and wish you could have that designer one to feel among too.

A need is that mobile phone you don't have; hence, your friends and parents can't reach you when they need to. Not having the phone also means you're missing out on important information. On the other hand, a want is that the latest version of the iPhone was just released a few days ago, and everyone on Twitter is talking about how cool it looks and feels.

Let's settle this matter once and for all. The best way to resolve the issue of need and want is to ask yourself some questions before you dole out the cash to pay for any item. Is this something I can do without? Is it something I can live without? If I don't have this item in a couple of days, weeks, months, and even years from now, would not having them hurt me?

If you can answer these questions frankly, you are well on your way to becoming financially wiser.

Although it feels good to have it, do you really need it?

## Your Financial Life is Important, Don't Leave it to Chance

Being a teenager and having a lot of time and years to play with sometimes gives you a false belief that you do not have to worry about your financial life. You tell yourself, it's one of those things that will take care of itself as you grow older; the only issue here is, it won't.

Sooner or later, you need to pay attention to your finances one way or the other. So, why not start now while it's still early? If you start now when it still looks early, you will avoid some financial blunders and start making better decisions from your lessons.

## How Teens Waste Money on Useless Items

Let's look at some of your useless expenses and how you can start making better decisions like a millionaire. The purpose of this section is not to make you believe that you have no right to enjoy now if you want to thrive financially. Not at all. You are young and you need to be happy and enjoy as much as you can. What is intended here is to boost your awareness against high dependency, exaggerations and unconsciousness in your expenses and habits. These can sometimes jeopardize your entire future.

## Parties and Alcohol

Parties, alcohol, and excessive entertainment are uncontrolled expenses that teens and millennials get involved in, and it eats deep into their pockets. Some even go as far as taking loans to host these parties and indulge in these entertainments. These habits have a way of gradually eating a hole into your finances; then, it becomes a big thing.

A recent study by Strutt & Parker revealed that millennials in the United Kingdom spend £3,016 ($4,135) every year just going out on the weekend. This cost is just for one person who hangs out for one night on the weekend and not the whole weekend.

Back to the reason why I combined alcohol and parties. When you go clubbing or to parties sober, you will not be in control of your spending. Alcohol is the trigger to uncontrolled spending due to its impact on your mind. It makes you have lesser control of your actions and expressions and, ultimately, spending. According to the NIH, large doses of alcohol cause temporary loss of memory. Even if you have never been in that situation, you must have heard of people who couldn't recall all they did the night before, all because they were drunk.

**Money Tip**: I would have said, stay away from alcohol completely, but I suspect you will not abide by that. So, my advice is, stop taking your credit card to parties and hang out with the girls or boys. Let's face it, parties and alcohol move together, such that when you start emptying the bottles into your system, you at the same time lose control of your system.

To avoid any surprises in the morning, leave your credit card at home and move with as little cash as possible.

Don't wake up in the morning and find yourself in huge debt. Wouldn't that be the real "After Party?"

## Expensive Coffee and Cigarettes

How many cups of coffee do you have in a day? I mean the one you pay for at your favorite coffee shop. Have you ever tried adding up the cost together to see what it comes to? I bet not. Let's try that here and now, but first, here's the price of coffee in a few cities around the world;

- In Canada, $4
- In Copenhagen, $6.24
- In Shanghai, $4.60
- In New York, $3.20
- In São Paulo, $1.50
- In Lagos, $0.62

These prices don't look much but let's say you drink up to 50 cups of coffee every month. If you live in Lagos, where the price on the list is the lowest, you will be spending $31 on coffee. In that part of the world, the average monthly salary is around $550. So, that is 6% of your income going to your favorite coffee maker. Try this calculation on your own to see what you arrive at.

Cigarettes have a similar effect on your pockets and income but even more far-reaching effects due to the health hazard it poses, which goes beyond the price of a packet. For example, in New York, a pack of cigarettes costs $14. How many packs do you smoke per week? Now work out the percentage against your income and see how much goes to the tobacco company from the hole in your pocket.

The health people keep saying that "smoking is dangerous for your health." The finance guys have since added their voice by saying, "the best way to save money is to quit smoking." Listen, I know it's not as easy as they make it sound, but how about we try something different to cut your cost? Try reducing the number of sticks you smoke by adopting cheaper alternatives to smoking and having it less frequently.

## Online Gambling/Betting

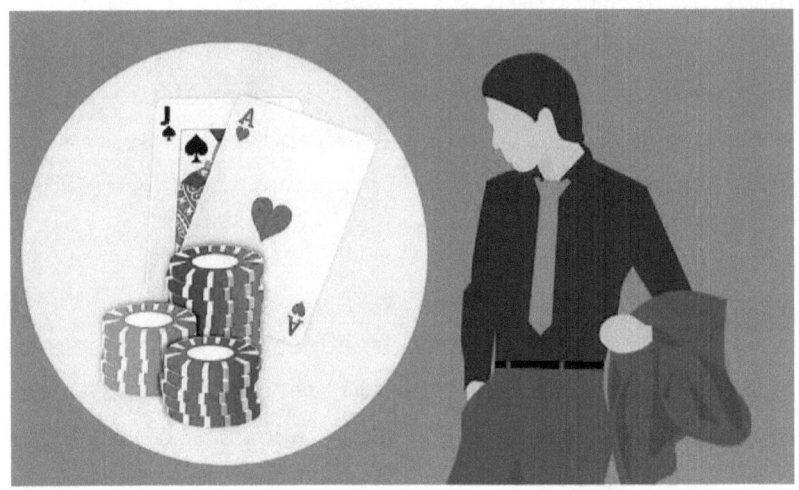

Still, in the study by Strutt and Parker, an average millennial spends £416 ($570.33). 30% of young people gamble at least once a month, with online gambling sites preferred to the brick and mortar locations. It is more of the same, if not trading bad for worse.

The danger of online gambling is even greater because there are no barriers. There has also been a deliberate swap in using the name "gambling" to 'betting." This is common with sports betting sites. They have also become more accessible in the form of apps on your mobile devices. The minimum deposits have also dropped to as low as $5 to $10 with promises of cash backs in some instances.

Online gambling is so popular among teenagers, and it is eating deep into your finances while you're not paying attention. You allow yourself to get carried away by the thrills and excitement, but in reality, you're wasting your money.

The only way you can spend less on gambling is not to gamble at all. If you are finding it difficult to quit, you need to start doing things differently. You can start by entrusting your funds with a reliable person like your parents, guardians, or friends, or simply take it to the bank and ask them about those types of accounts where you don't have easy access to the money. That may even be the beginning of something big for your finances. Also, try to have only the money you need for your basic needs at any time, like money for food, transportation, and for paying utility bills.

The number of teenagers who have become millionaires from hard work far outnumbers those who have made it from gambling. I just thought to put that out here.

## Fake Status

It is known that teenagers would rather have the latest branded item on their shopping list than think about buying a home or going into a real estate investment business. Also, buying a home is still out of the reach of young people; they would prefer to go for items that boost their status on social media or something else to feed their self-esteem. Instead, teens would rather spend money on items they can show off on social media to brag to their followers than think or talk about investments.

Social media is one of the primary reasons why teenagers waste money on fake lives and status items like the latest iPhones, Prada, Chanel, Balenciaga, and others, just to show off. According to Statista.com, more than 64% of young adults in the U.S. use Instagram. This same Instagram that is very popular among teenagers has been identified as the most harmful network for your mental health.

It's almost impossible to avoid being wasteful if you stay glued to Instagram because you will want to follow suit in bragging about something. IG, as it is fondly called, is where you see young people flaunting large sums of cash; meanwhile, in real life, they are struggling to feed. Same place you find your favorite influencers who keep recommending products they have never used to you because they have been paid to make you buy them, and brands keep tempting you to spend on the next new thing, which has very little difference and value than the previous version. It's a cruel, crazy world out there on social media.

Most people on social media only show off their best moments and their fake lives; they do not show you their struggles. If you want to be richer, you have to stop wasting money on trends and fads. Pull yourself out of this wrecking train and ignore the delusive fear of missing out. The next time you want to buy anything, pause and ask yourself, "Is this a need or a want?" If the purpose of that purchase is to take selfies and show off on IG, then you do not need that item.

## Multi-devices with The Same Function

One of the emerging habits that are fast-growing among teenagers is the need to own multiple devices that perform the same functions. For example, a teenager can own an iPad, iPhone, iPod, a tablet, Personal Digital Assistant, an Xbox, and a PlayStation, all at the same time. That is not all; they can have recurring subscriptions on all these devices.

This might sound like an extreme incident, but a lot of you fall into this same category. All these devices serve the same purposes, but you feel the need to have them, and you don't know you are wasting money keeping them.

## In-game Purchases

In-game purchases are by the far top on the list of "money-wasters" for teens. Recall how you were having fun with your game? You got to this new level never achieved before, but suddenly you failed the level. Something in you tells you that you can make it to the next level while the game requires you to make an in-app payment to continue. You most likely will go ahead and make that payment. How many of those payments have you made on different games?

Video games of any form are the ultimate hobby for teenagers and millennials, and big corporations have identified the impulsive buying nature of young people. They are pushing more offers to you like never seen before.

If you want to be a rich teenager, you need to cut down on these purchases and control your impulse when it's time to make a payment of any form. Remember what we said about what you need and what you want?

Stop the waste today. Start a new day by taking charge of your finances. Free yourself from the shackles of these wastes and start doing things differently.

This is by no means suggesting you should not have fun. Not at all! That's not what I'm saying. After all, there are more cost-effective ways to have fun without blowing away your dreams.

*Chapter 2*

# Money Basics – Making, Saving and Spending Money

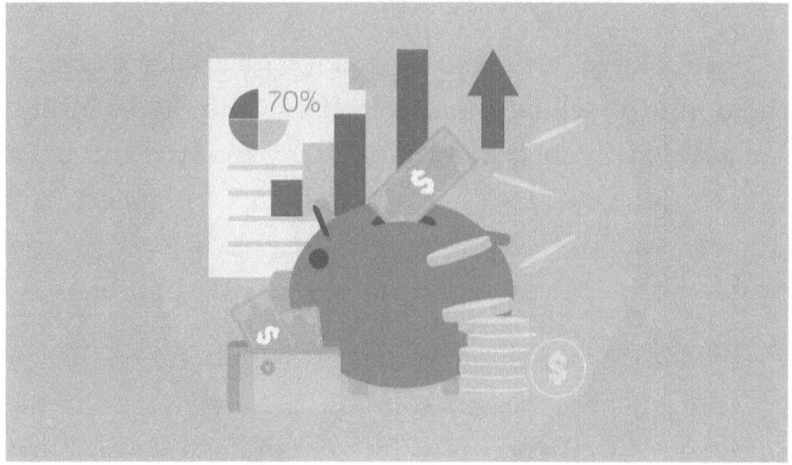

Remember how we started in the previous chapter? It's all about your mindset and attitude. If you have the right attitude and mindset about money, it would not matter if you were a pre-teen or a teenager; you will make good money and become richer.

After that, you may still be dealing with some doubts about what you need to do to start earning right away. There are loads of ideas out there you can try, but the most important thing is to solve problems.

Look around you; there are problems all over the place in need of people to solve them.

Christian saw the challenges users of MacBook had with the cost of multiple apps and offered a solution by bundling apps for a lesser price. This solution that looked like a regular thing anyone could have done made him a lot of money and helped him start his first company in his early teenage years.

Emil Motycka started by picking golf balls, cleaning them, and reselling them to golfers. Then later in life, he mowed his uncle's lawn for $10. From the golf balls to lawn mowing, Emil solved problems for golfers, his uncles, and the neighbors. Today, he is still solving problems for people, and they are paying him big.

So, look around you and your neighborhood; yours could even be a virtual solution. I want you to know someone is waiting and willing to pay for that problem you are willing to help them solve. From one person, it will multiply to tens and hundreds and thousands of people willing to pay big money for your solution.

## Start Making Money Now

As a teenager, you can stop collecting money from your parents or expect money from them, especially if you're the type that likes to be independent. There are tons of jobs designed for teenagers that you can do to start making your own money right away.

Whatever your love and passion are, there's something out there that fits you, and you can make money from it. If you have the love and passion for the virtual world, jobs like surveys, teaching, and skills transfer, among others, are available online, and you can start right away. If you don't have a lot of time in your hands, summer jobs designed for teens are waiting for you.

Guess what? If you feel you are not cut out for all these jobs out there, or you're not willing to work for anyone, you can create your own thing. That's what being a young person is all about. You have time in your hands. So, be like other teens like you and use that time and create your own thing.

You could do so well in your work or business to the point where you can buy yourself a car and all the good things you have ever desired when you start making money yourself. You can be free and never have to rely on anyone ever again. You could even start investing for your future now and watch your money multiply year after year.

Most importantly, whether you choose to pick a job or start your own business, starting right away will give you a massive advantage over many. You will start learning some critical business and life lessons that can only be gathered from experience. These lessons you're learning will make you better every day, and before you even know it, you are not only more prosperous but more innovative and more intelligent.

Whatever you choose to do, please start it now! Procrastination never makes anyone better; it only kills dreams.

Let me show you how to make money from side hustles without having to drop out of school. From online opportunities to small business ideas, you can make money with or without a job as a teenager.

## Start Blogging

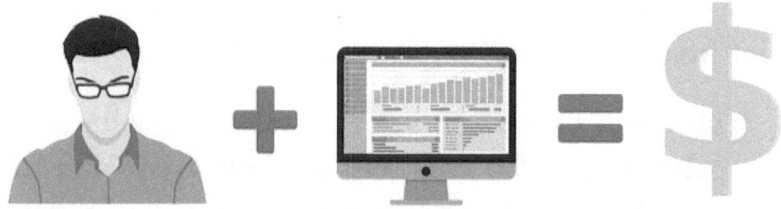

Blogging is a fun way fun teenagers can make money because there are several topics you can talk about. You will be surprised at the number of people interested in what you have to say. Although it's not an easy way to make money, it's a famous work-from-home side gig that will eventually bring in the cash.

Your first dime as a blogger might take some time to come, but you have to remain consistent in dishing out content. Blogging is a fun way of making money because it's enjoyable for those who blog, and the money will follow with time.

Another cool thing about being a blogger is that it can lead to you writing your first book, which you can then sell on Amazon and other platforms. Writing books is another fun source of income. This book you are reading will continue to bring income for our company for a long time to come in sales and royalty, but most importantly, it's solving a problem, and it's available globally.

## Start Taking Surveys

Over the years, the popularity of survey sites has dropped due to the bad reputation they have been getting, linking them to scams. However, there are still several legit survey sites where you can make great money regularly. You need to know how to find them.

Surveys may not offer a lot of money at once, but they are still one of the easiest ways to find money anywhere because you can fill out surveys within a few minutes while lying on your bed or before your movie on Netflix or YouTube.

Here are some of the best sites where teenagers can make money taking surveys (take note of the age limits).

- **E-Poll** (Age 13 upwards): They conduct surveys about sports, celebrities, and entertainment.

- **Swagbucks** (Age 13 upwards): This is perhaps the most trusted of them all. They have paid more than $330 million to users since inception.

- **Treasure Trooper** (Age 13 upwards): Their surveys are centered around games and Questions and Answers about some topics.

- **Survey Junkie** (Age 13 upwards): The surveys on this site are often short, and they pay well too.

- **My Points** (Age 13 upwards): You can make money reading emails, watching videos, and more.

- **VIP Voice** (Age 13 upwards for U.S. and Age 18 upwards for Canada): you earn points that can be used to enter sweepstakes.

- **Toluna** (Age 13 upwards): You can earn money by filling surveys and referring your friends.

## Be a Virtual Teacher

Who would have thought virtual teaching would be a thing in high demand? The recent Covid19 pandemic has forced the world to reset the way we all work, and suddenly teachers are now in high demand.

Due to several lockdown regulations, parents and guardians require teachers to keep their young ones busy or help them with their missing lessons while their schools remain locked. So, if you have expertise in certain subjects, now is the time to make money with them.

There are platforms online looking for teachers in various subjects and even teenagers who can teach their mates one skill or the other. You need to put yourself out there, and someone will find you.

## Take Up a Job at a Restaurant

Look around you; restaurants and sit-down food establishments are constantly springing up here and there, always needing teenagers to manage some roles like cash registers, waiters/waitresses, and hostesses. If you have some experience, you might even get higher roles in the kitchen or other departments.

Depending on the size and set-up of the establishments, you could be asked to make deliveries; you can even get some added advantages if you are licensed to drive. The benefits from this type of job are numerous. You get to take home at least a minimum wage. If you are good at your jobs, you can get tips from clients and your bosses, and you can enjoy free or discounted food.

Ultimately, your experience is expanding, your resume is looking better, and don't forget the part where you will be earning some income.

## Offer Snow Service

A snow service sounds like a good business idea if you live in a cold area. People typically avoid cleaning the snow out of their driveways because of the stress involved and avoid exposing themselves to the cold weather. You can take advantage of the situation and offer to shovel the snow out of their driveways for a fee. To avoid running out of clients, you can set up a rotation of your clients.

This is a superb way of making some cool cash without investing too much in working tools.

## Offer Lawn and Landscaping Services

Mowing and landscaping will be a great way of making money for teenagers because adults are too busy doing their lawn, but they want it neat and clean. Also, mowing and landscaping are labor-intensive and the perfect job for a teenager like you. If you get the hang of it, mowing can be fun and a reasonable means of getting some extra income.

You could also offer to plant garden beds for some clients, rake leaves, clean their dogs, and water their landscapes. You just need to be creative in the services you are offering.

Mowing and landscaping jobs are readily available in your neighborhood. If you get good at it, you could get a regular, steady income from it and possibly turn it into something bigger like Emil Motycka did.

## Provide Babysitting Services

Babysitting has always been a good way for teenagers to start earning extra income. You can start with family and friends, and the word will spread in the community before you know it. Alternatively, you could print flyers and share them within your community to inform them about your services. I can bet some parents will interview you right there on the spot.

This type of service has a way of spreading through word-of-mouth, and you will be surprised how much you can make per hour. The standard rate for a babysitter is $10 per hour plus $3 for an additional child. A lot of parents even provide meals for the babysitter.

Another money-making opportunity in this line is by being a parent helper. In this instance, you are not home alone with the children but supporting the parents in activities like playing with the children, folding clothes, and other activities.

## Photography and Video Editing Services

I know your first thought would be that everyone takes pictures on their mobile phones and stores them there. Yes, you're probably right. However, the fact remains that if you are good at taking great pictures at events or good at editing pictures to make them look amazing, that could be a business opportunity for you.

People are constantly looking for people who are better photographers to help them capture moments in their lives. Imagine if you now throw in video editing into the mix; that would be something special. Photography and video editing are some of the best paying jobs for teenagers and adults. So, it's time to put those photoshopping skills to proper use and start making money with them.

## Become a Coach

Being a coach in a little league can be a fun way of earning money as a teenager. Many schools in your community or neighboring community might need an experienced junior coach to help them coach the next generation. This could be an opportunity to earn some good cash while having fun and becoming a role model to several young people or the entire team.

So, even if you never made your high school team, you could still use your little experience to earn some money while having fun.

## Become a Golf Caddy

Being a caddy requires you to carry the golfer's bag and follow them around the golf course to any point the golf ball goes until they finish playing for the day. That's all that is required of you as a rookie caddy. Then you get paid at the end of the day.

Isn't that a terrific way to earn some nice income?

## Make Money Working in Retail

Retail jobs are other jobs readily available for teenagers. They involve operating cash registers, talking to customers, and stocking shelves. In addition to getting paid, this is a great learning experience.

Most retail jobs offer a minimum wage, and if you impress their organization, you get a raise and more bonuses, like tuition assistance for long-term employees.

Carry out thorough research and see if you can find retailers that offer benefits and the opportunity to transfer to a different store when you leave school.

## Become a Gym Assistant

If you are already a "fit fam" and enjoy spending time in the gym, maybe it's time to put that passion to more use and start making money. You can ask your local gym for a job. Most gyms will allow you to work out for free. That is free membership plus a paycheck.

Also, sports centers are always in need of teenagers for some jobs like ball boys and girls to help with stray balls, among other duties. These jobs will go a long way in boosting your finances.

## Pet Sitting Services

Petting is a great way to make money as a teenager if you love pets. There are pet owners all over the place who require people to play with their pets. For example, depending on the part of the world and your experience, some dog walkers earn up to $50 per hour. Others just need you to watch their cats while they are away.

This can be a cool way to make some money, especially if you are a pet lover. You can send out flyers in your neighborhood informing them of your services. Also, you can let the local pet shop and clinic know what you offer and leave some flyers with them.

Rover.com is one of the most reliable platforms to find pet sitting jobs. Sign up, enter your area code and see all the locals who are looking for pet sitters. The potential of having repeat and regular patronage is high with pet sitting jobs.

## Become a House Sitter

Like pet sitting, some people need someone to watch over their home while traveling out of town on vacation or for a couple of days. Your job in the house might include walking their dogs, picking up mail, mowing the lawn, and a few other tasks. Some homeowners will allow you to sleep over till they arrive, while others are okay with you stopping by every couple of days.

You can start this type of job by informing your family and friends about your availability; gradually, you can move into spreading the word through printed flyers. Alternatively, you can create a profile on one of the numerous platforms online. Most of the platforms allow you to register for free but charge a tiny percentage of your income.

House sitting is one of the best jobs for teenagers because it pays well, and you spend almost nothing while doing it.

## House and Garage Cleaning

For teenagers who have a knack for cleanliness and organization, you can exchange that energy and passion for cash. There are families all over the country with overflowing garages and disorganized homes who need your service.

Decide how you want to charge, either a flat fee or by the size of the house. Alternatively, you could join an already thriving company. That way, you will not have to struggle with finding clients yourself.

## Stream on Twitch.tv

Twitch.tv is an online platform where people stream themselves playing video games or having general conversations live. Streamers have followers like any other social media platform. Also, as a streamer, you can make money from ads, donations, subscribers, tips, and more.

For example, popular Twitchers like "Ninja" make millions of dollars by live-streaming several games and other events on the platform.

So, are you thinking what I'm thinking? It's time to put your gaming skills to good use and start making money with them. Start live streaming today and let other people join and watch you play. You could also use that opportunity to show off some skills and share some "cheats" you've learned.

## Neighborhood Car Wash Services

If you live in a community where the people have a lot of cars, you can decide to start running a home service car wash where you offer to wash these cars at the home of the owners. You will be surprised at how many people will be interested in having their cars washed while they remain in the comfort of their houses.

As long as the houses have a water spigot, you should be fine. The other tools you will need to carry are rags, soap, a sponge, and other items you need to wash a car. It will be an added advantage if you know how to drive because you will move the cars to your spot of choice.

## Start Selling Stuff at School

Suppose you are serious about making your own money and becoming financially independent. In that case, you will need to get over your "shyness" and start selling in your school because it is one of the best and fastest ways to start making money. It's the same old-school method of buying and selling.

Remember what we said earlier, your money is in the problem you help people solve. So, look around your school and find a problem you can solve. Sometimes it's as simple as selling candy, gums, soda/energy drinks, while in some cases, it would require you to use your soft skills to create a solution for your fellow students.

So, start thinking now, look around and come up with a solution. You may need to ask your friends and tell them to ask their friends about what you consider before you start selling them.

## Become a Summer Camp Counselor

Perhaps you are only available to work during the summer; being a camp counselor is an excellent choice to take on as a job. Parents send their children to several boot camps, and the camps always need teenagers to work as counselors. So, you will be working with a group of children, and it can be enjoyable.

## Make Money Running Errands

This is probably the oldest known job for teenagers. If you know places in your community and you have the time, you can offer to run errands like picking up groceries, mails, newspapers, cleaning, and others for a fee.

It would help your community know you offer this service and the time you will be available to run the errands. Make your fees clear, and if possible, offer a discount for combined errands along the same routes.

## Be a Certified Lifeguard

The job of a lifeguard involves safety around the pool and sea area. To get paid well as a lifeguard, you need to pass the certification exam. Lifeguards get paid more than minimum wages because their responsibilities involve saving lives. That's one of the reasons it's one of the coolest jobs for teenagers.

## Teach Children Coding

Maybe you are already a computer geek with expertise in coding; you can offer to teach the young ones this invaluable skill physically or online. Coding and other computer skills tend to attract many clients; parents will be willing to pay a premium so their children can learn the skills.

You can teach other subjects like drawing, music instruments, storytelling, sports and a whole lot more.

## Consider Selling Pleasure Foods

If you are a fantastic baker, you may want to consider setting up shop at the farmers' market, where you can show off your baking skills within the community. Cakes, cookies, and other exceptional food attract customers. All food-related businesses have the potential of turning into something bigger within a short time.

While doing this, you will quickly learn how to charge, calculate your margin and turnover. You will be learning how to run a successful baking business.

## Flipping Items to Make Money

As a teen, you can quickly learn how to make money by flipping items. Start from your home by asking your parents or guardians if they no longer need items but will be willing to sell them at a profit.

Next, use that extra cash to get other fast-moving items like electronics, gadgets, books, and game consoles and sell them for a profit. Guess what? What you are doing is what some big-name real estate businessmen do, just on a larger scale.

## Sell Creative Items on Etsy

Suppose you are creative with your hands and enjoy crafting items like printable cards, baths, body products, jewelry, and others. As a teen, you can literally make a lot of money making crafts you can sell online and learn how to manage a business while at it.

## Start Vlogging

For those who are not camera-shy, vlogging, which is the video version of blogging, could be a great way to make money as teenagers. You can set up a channel on platforms like YouTube and get paid while people come to watch and comment on your videos. If you wonder what the content would be, look around you; there's a problem that needs a solution; talk about it. Offer people more straightforward and better ways of doing even the things they already knew before.

Evan was already reviewing toys at age 8 with the help of his parents. You can do better; you just didn't know it because you have not started. There are thousands of topics you can talk about to start making money. Viewers are often attracted to vloggers who are natural and make them feel important and a part of their lives.

Now, look into the camera and try something today; the world is waiting for your content.

## Get Paid to Have Fun

Teenagers are typically gamers, so why not get paid to play games? After all, you're already spending long hours playing games, and no one is paying you for it. Platforms like Swagbucks have been paying gamers for many years. All they need you to do is play selected games and give your feedback or watch videos.

Several sites also pay game testers to try out their games and get feedback before they are officially released. You will be surprised how much you can carry out this task, especially if your feedback helps the company significantly.

## Make Money By Installing These Apps

For teenagers who can't do without multiple devices, some platforms are willing to pay you for installing apps on your multiple devices. The purpose is to collect data like the apps you use the most, your games, and other information. It's generally harmless information they are collecting and willing to pay for it.

Below are some of the apps you can get started with right away;

- SurveySavvy (Pays $60 to $190 per year): Pays $5 per month for each connected device and allows up to three devices. You can earn up to $180 a year.

- Smart Panel (Pays $60 plus per year): Pays $5 per month if your PC, tablet, or mobile phone stays connected. Additionally, they pay a loyalty bonus every quarter as long as your device stays connected.

These amounts may look insignificant but don't forget that you are not required to do anything more than stay connected and get paid.

## Learn a Profitable Skill

Teenage years are the best time to learn a skill because you have all the time to do so and all the time to start putting them to use to make money. The earlier you learn some skills, the faster your cash can start coming in.

Below are some money-making skills you can consider learning;

- Social Media Management
- Coding
- Freelance writing (Ghostwriting)
- Blockchain and Cryptocurrency
- Digital Marketing
- Customer Service management
- Transcribing and Translating
- Bookkeeping

The list is endless, and quite a number of them are available for free if you know how to navigate the internet to find what you want. The better you get at your skill of choice, the more clients will be willing to pay for your service.

Practice the skills you have learned and get better at them. Ask your family and friends for honest feedback and make the necessary adjustments. Then go ahead and set up a freelancing account on any of the platforms available out there.

Here's a list of some of the top freelancing platforms where you can start offering your skills.

- Upwork
- Fiverr
- Freelancer.com
- PeoplePerHour
- Toptal
- 99designs
- Behance
- Flexjobs

You will be surprised at how much some people make from the comfort of their homes. You can even do better because you have age and time at your disposal.

## Get a Part-time Job

Part-time jobs are readily available, and teenagers who are willing will find something interesting that pays. While the payments from part-time jobs might not be high, the experience will always be worth it.

Here's a list of some part-time jobs for teens you can find around your community;

- **Pizza Delivery**: It seems this job was created with teenagers in mind. It's a classic teen's job. Depending on the nature of the delivery task, you may need a license for it.

- **Grocery Stores**: Grocery stores are always hiring so you stand a good chance of landing a job in one.

- **Movie Theatres:** this is another classic place to find part-time jobs. They are always in need of teenagers to operate their food and ticketing stands.

- **Parks and Amusement Places**: This is another type of job that suits you as a teenager. You will find many of your age grades working at amusement parks. Plus, the environment is fun.

- **Referee**: If you know the rules of a particular game very well, you could offer to be a referee, a judge, or an umpire. Players are in high demand, but referees are not. So, this could be a cool way to earn some income.

The list of part-time jobs you can land is endless. Check your local listing and online job boards to find something that works for you. The goal is to gather as much experience while getting paid.

## Make Money By Renting Your Stuff

There are some items you have in excess that you're not using anymore, like game DVDs, consoles, books, bikes, scooters, soccer balls, basketball, and others. You can start renting them for a little cash here and there. There are young people in your community whose parents are unwilling to buy these things for them but will be willing to rent them from you.

You can charge a flat fee or an hourly fee. Whatever method you decide, try to record all your items, who rented what, the due date, and the amount paid. You could introduce a penalty for late returns.

## Sell Stock Photos

If you have a good eye for creative images, there are platforms like Shutterstock, iStock, and Getty Images, among others, where you can get paid for your images. As long as the images are great, you will get paid every time someone downloads them.

This is another fantastic way a teenager can make money without stress. If you have been complimented for your photography skills a couple of times by your friends and family, maybe it's time to make money with that skill.

I have deliberately provided you with several options to choose from, and trust me, this list is not even close to all the jobs you can find or start on your own as a teenager. Also, I know all these jobs don't look like life-transforming jobs that will make you millions. The point is, it's not the job that will make them millions but you, your attitude, and your mindset. These jobs will provide you with the required experience to start something little that will turn out great in a few years.

## Tips to Help You on the Job

I want to close this chapter with these few tips:

- Expect to make mistakes. When you start something new, you are likely to make mistakes. It's all part of the process. Don't get discouraged, instead figure out what went wrong and have a go at it again and again until you get the best result. Never let your mistakes discourage or define you; instead, use them as stepping blocks to your success.

- Have Fun. Whatever you've decided to do for money, it is best when you have fun doing it. Look for the best way to enjoy it. After all, that's one of the benefits of being a teenager; you love to have fun. So, do that while making money.

- Deliver only the best. Recall how I mentioned a couple of times that your money is in the solution you're providing? It's true! Make sure to do your best and only deliver the best to your clients. Your quality will be noticed, and it will make you stand out. People are always willing to pay more for premium quality. Give it a shot from now on, and you will see the result.

- Be Creative. At about age 7, my dad gave me his version of the definition of a genius. He said, "A genius is not someone that invented something but the person that made that invention unique and useful to other people." I can't forget that in a long time. Use all these ideas mentioned in this book as stepping stones to create unique solutions. The more unique your product is, the more patronage you will enjoy and the better your chance of success.

- Start Now! As you close this book, go out there and start right away—no more excuses. Millions of adults wish they had this rare opportunity you have. They didn't have anyone to guide them, and some are still struggling as we speak. Now is the best time you have if you want to be wealthy and financially independent.

*Chapter 3*

# Savings & Banking – Strategies for Growing Your Wealth

When you start working, money will definitely start coming your way. If you decide to cut down on those mistakes mentioned earlier, you will have even more money than you ever imagined. So, what do you do with all the money you will be making when you start to work? I can imagine you rolling your eyes at this question because you have a thousand and one things on your list. That's fine.

However, what about trying something different that can make you richer for a long time? This is one of the secrets of the rich. Every millionaire pre-teen and teenager you know practices this habit, but you don't know; that's why I'm revealing it to you here and now. If I have to teach anything in any school across the globe today, it will be about saving because I know it's a secret that can make you more prosperous and even more affluent.

Saving means putting a portion of your money away for a rainy day. It involves putting away some part of your earnings in the bank, in a piggy, or an investment account. This practice is not a one-time event but a reoccurring one. That is why the phrase "Saving Culture" or a "Saving Habit" is commonly used to refer to your savings. Your saving habit is the foundation of your wealth. It's nearly impossible to be as rich as you desire without you learning this habit.

## Reasons Why You Need to Start Saving Today

The reasons you need to develop or improve your saving habits are numerous. I will be discussing a few of them here so you can have an idea why this is important to you becoming a rich young person. So, let's get right into it.

## You Would be Learning Financial Literacy

Financial literacy is one of the critical subjects that are still not widely taught in many schools across the globe. However, it remains an essential topic that if young people learn it early enough, they will make better financial decisions as they grow up.

Learning to save will give you a natural ability in your personal finance because being someone who doesn't spend all is vital for managing your expenses, big purchases, and wealth-building. If you fail to learn this habit, you will struggle with your plans, and it won't be easy to stay diligent while paying your bills will become challenging. You will even find it challenging to save for important events like holidays and buying a home when the time comes.

## It's Your Path to Independence and Self-reliance

A saving culture is one of the fastest paths to becoming financially independent until you become an adult. For example, if you want to make a big purchase, let's say a car. You certainly do not have the money to buy it now, but you can start saving gradually until you can afford it.

What that does for you is teach you how to be responsible and independent because you are not planning on asking anyone for money but rather save towards achieving that goal. The more money you save towards your goal, the more your confidence grows, and soon you will understand the power you have and use it better all the time. Here's a secret: If you can save to buy something small, you will be able to save to buy something even bigger. Try it out today.

## Helps You Spend Wisely

An excellent saving culture and budgeting can help you develop the financial discipline you need to achieve your dreams. It can also help you in other areas of your life if you apply it accordingly. When you practice this habit more often, it will quickly become natural and a way of life for you. A saving culture will help you understand better the difference between want and need.

Money will always be limited, and your wants will always be more than what you're earning. So, savings can teach you other strategies to get your desired item, like trade-offs and opportunity costs. All these will lead you to make better spending choices. You will better judge what is a good thing to spend money on and ultimately avoid impulse spending.

When you set saving goals and work towards achieving them, you feel this sense of satisfaction and believe that you can do it over and over again, even with bigger dreams.

## Help Prepare You for Access to Financial Products

When you develop a saving habit as a teen, it prepares you for what is to come regarding access to a wide range of financial products. When you are 18+ in most countries, you start to have access to financial products like credit cards, mobile phone contracts, and payday loans. It would be best if you were financially responsible and independent before all these come your way so you can make the best decisions.

Access to some of these products often makes some young people believe free money has come their way. This type of thinking has led many to incur debts they will continue to pay for a long time to come. However, if you have developed a good saving habit before 18, you will make better decisions when these accesses come your way.

## You Can Achieve Your Financial Goals

Learning to save teaches you how to set money goals, build your wealth, and do things you can to achieve your financial goals faster. It also helps plan for the future and all the great things you need money to achieve. Anyone who doesn't practice a saving culture is only thinking about their immediate needs today.

They are not looking beyond now. I'm sure you don't want to be that type of person. So, plan to look ahead, starting with a few weeks, then three months; that way, a long-term plan will be much easier to achieve. If you check out any of these rich young people, you will notice a pattern with them; they all have financial dreams and targets for the future.

Start developing great traits like planning, setting goals, and delayed gratification. Write out your list, then rearrange them according to importance (don't forget wants and needs), then set out a plan to start achieving these goals in order of importance.

## Tips to Improve Your Saving Culture

Now that I have your attention, I'm sure you are now thinking about the strategies you can adopt to start saving a lot better than you were doing before. I will leave you with a few tips to help you make your thinking easier. Below are some strategies you can implement to improve your saving culture.

1. The first obvious strategy will be increasing your earnings because your savings will also see a boost if you can increase your earnings. There are a few things you can do to make this happen.

    - Ask for cash gifts on a special occasion like your birthday and other special events in your life. To avoid coming off as ungrateful, let your folks know you are saving for a big purchase.

- Check with your parents or guardians to get a cash raise for doing extra chores around the house. You can extend the same to your neighbors.

- Check the house for items that are no longer in use, then confirm with your parents if you can sell them for some cash to add to your savings.

- If you already have a job and feel you are doing a great job, it would be easier to ask your employer for a raise. Better still, you could ask for a higher role with better pay.

  Companies often prefer to move people up from within rather than bring in a new person.

- Search for a better-paying job. This is easier when you already have an impressive resume. Sometimes, you never know what's out there until you search.

- Check online for extra jobs where you can invest your free time in exchange for some money.

2. Save a more significant portion of your earnings. This strategy requires some planning, budgeting, and discipline. You don't want to deprive yourself of the excellent and essential things of life in the name of saving for the future. We need you in good condition to manage the wealth you're building. Here are a few things you can do.

- Write out all your subscription services, rank them out in order of priority, then strike out the ones you can do without so the money you're saving from them can go into your savings.

- Reduce the expenses you carry out on your credit cards. These cards attract interest, and sometimes they can eat deeper into your finances and put you in a bad place.

  Consider making some cash payments and living within your means.

- Avoid impulsive buying. Avoid being in a hurry to spend your hard-earned money. If you need to buy something, take time to shop around for the best prices and deals. There are several times in the year when big sales happen, like Black Fridays, Vet Days, Christmas, and other high discount times of the year. Delay your purchases to make the most out of these discounts sales.

- Some items you want to buy have a student discount, and if you don't ask, you may not know. So, take time to ask if the sellers offer any form of discount, including students. Any form of saving you can get is good for you and should go into your savings.

3. Save for a more extended period. When you have a target for a big purchase, take time to save for that

item. Sometimes patience pays, and you may see a price crash that works in your favor.

4. Check for some cheaper options. If you have a big purchase like a car on your budget, then saving for a brand new one might take a long time and almost empty your entire savings, but it becomes reasonable and achievable if you consider the prices of fairly used cars.

These strategies and more will help you save more and build sustainable wealth for the future. Remember what we said earlier; it is more about attitude and mindset. If these two are correct, you will find the will and ways to save better, and in no time, you will start living your dreams.

## Teens Guide to Banking & Financial Products

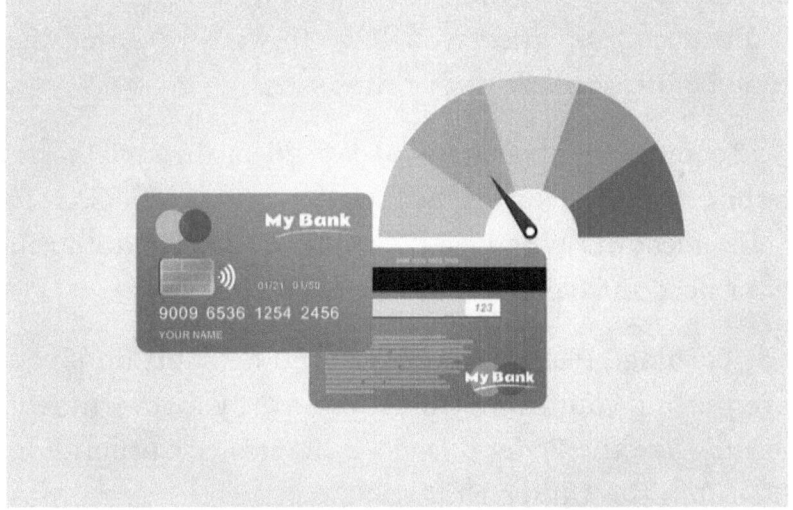

The more you start to make money and set out on your path to being rich, the more likely you will need to interact with the bank more often. Once you start making money, you need to start banking. I'm aware that the topic of banking is a little boring to some of you because of the jargon involved, but I will try to make it simple for you because you can't do without the bank if you're going to build your wealth.

Let's look at some basic terms and banking products you will need very soon if you are not already using them;

## Deposit

Deposit is the term used to explain the act of putting money into an account. When you add money to your account, you are making a deposit, which means the bank is keeping the money in trust for you, and you can come for it any time you desire. However, there are a few accounts where you have to wait for a specific time before accessing your funds.

To make a deposit, you can do it through cash, online transfer, direct deposit, or pay a check into your account. When you deposit into your account, your account balance increases positively.

Warning: Please ensure that the institution you are putting your money in is insured by a government agency like the Federal Deposit Insurance Corporation (FDIC) in the United States.

## Withdrawal

Withdrawal is the flip side of a deposit. It is the term used to describe the act of taking money out of your account. When you make a deposit, the only way to get the money out of your bank account is through withdrawal. Withdrawal can happen electronically, at the ATM, or by visiting the bank to make a physical withdrawal.

## Types of Bank Accounts

These days, banks have created several types of products to make banking services accessible for their customers. Ultimately, however, all of these products serve the same purpose. So, let's look at the basic types of accounts available in banks that teens can take advantage of and start using today.

## Savings Accounts

Savings accounts are the most basic type of account you can open in a bank. The requirements are not complex, and you can start with small amounts. However, there's a limit to the number of times you can withdraw from most savings accounts. Some banks will place a limit of four to six times a month on withdrawals. Anything above that, you will forfeit the interest that would have been added to your balance. The purpose of savings accounts is to encourage savings habits.

## Checking Accounts

This type of account has no restrictions on withdrawals. You can deposit and take out your fund at any time. You can even get a checkbook which you can use to write a paycheck to pay other people. The holders of your paycheck can cash it or pay it into their account anytime they desire, as long as it has your signature on it.

## Investment Accounts

Banks offer several types of investment accounts, but they are long-term savings accounts where you can grow your money in most cases. An investment account can help you achieve the goal of building your wealth. Investment account yields returns over time, which increases the value of your investment or dividends.

When you have a future purchase like a car, home, or even retirement, then an investment account is what you need. An investment account is where your money starts to work for you while you focus on other things. More about investments later.

## Money Apps: Cashapp, PayPal, Stripe, Venmo

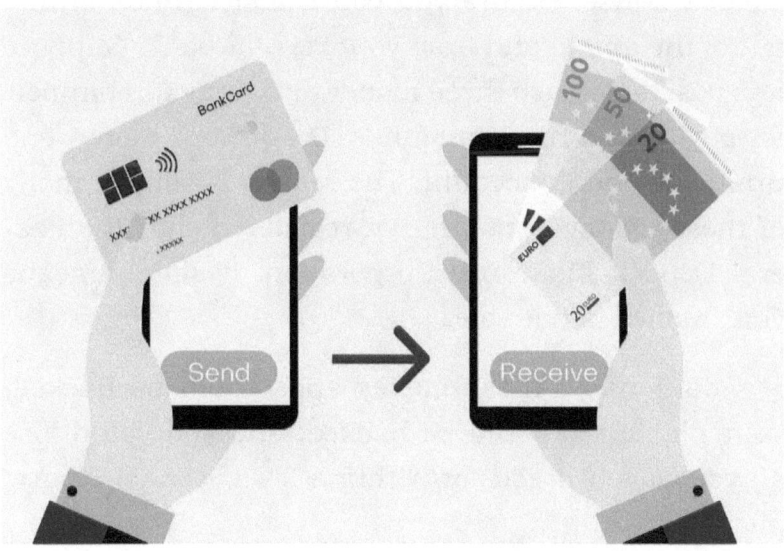

Over the years, the way we carry out banking has been changing almost daily. Previously, you needed to get to the ATM, the physical bank, or at best use the internet to carry out banking transactions. All that looks like the stone age now because Money Apps have taken over all that. From the comfort of your home and by tapping a few buttons, you carry out a banking transaction from your room to the farthest country you can imagine.

As a working teen, I strongly encourage the use of money apps, especially to get paid. Money apps make payment very fast and effective. You can complete a task and get pain right away while waiting for confirmation from your bank.

**Just a little warning:** Whichever money app you choose to use, ensure you can transfer funds in and out of the app to and from your regular bank. Suppose it is possible to use these money apps only as channels for paying and receiving funds. Let all your money end up in your bank account. The reason is simple: many of these money apps are not registered with the Federal Deposit Insurance Corporation. It simply means your money is not safe.

Additionally, these money apps could be hacked, your phone too could be hacked, and you could lose all you have worked for within a few seconds. Please, play it safe.

## Banking Fees

Banks exist to safeguard your funds and provide you with other services you require of them, but these services are not free of charge. Even with the transition from brick-and-mortar banking to mobile app banking, the charges have not changed much because banks still rake in billions every year in charges and declare big profits.

As pre-teens and teenagers just starting banking activities, you need to be aware of the charges involved for every banking service you are carrying out. The quickest way to lose money is through bank charges because the bank will not ask your permission to take the charges from your account; they just go ahead and take it. Some of the fees you need to watch out for include transfer fees, deposit fees, and an overdraft.

## How You Spend Your Money

The emergence of digital banking has sent cash to the back burner on the list of most used means of payment. At the top of the list are bank cards, money apps, and internet transfers. Let's break it down further;

### Cash

Cash is the oldest and most reliable means of payment. Many teens who mostly rely on digital banking immediately return to cash when the apps fail them. The risk with cash is that the more cash you carry, the more you risk losing them because there's no protection for you and your money. It will be challenging to track your transactions and stick to a budget with a cash payment arrangement. Platforms like Amazon, DoorDash, Uber, and others do not accept cash payments, so it may not be easy to use them. Cash transactions are often untraceable, and that's not good for your saving habit.

### Debit Cards

When you open a checking or savings account with a bank, you will be issued debit cards to make a withdrawal from your account easier. It also makes your online transactions easier. You can go to any ATM nearby to withdraw money using your debit card.

With your debit card, you can withdraw your money only and nothing more than that. Occasionally, banks approve you to withdraw more than you have in your account; it is called an overdraft, and it comes with charges. Also, take note that debit cards attract monthly or annual fees, among others.

## Credit Cards

Unlike debit cards, banks allow you to spend more than what you have in your account and then expect you to pay it back within a specific period. Credit card spending attracts interest charges, so you need to be careful with them. When you fail to pay back the bank's money, they will charge a penalty fee and interest.

One of the benefits of the credit card is that it's protected against fraud and unauthorized usage. Also, your bank will report your credit habit to the credit bureau. The better your credit history, the more money you are likely to attract and at a lower rate. On the flip side, if you have a terrible habit of not paying what you had spent on time, you will have a poor record, making it challenging to access better interest rates and principal amounts.

Teenagers should do everything required to keep their credit scores as high as possible because you never know when you will need more funds for your business.

Understanding the concept of savings and the benefits, along with basic banking knowledge, is very crucial to your mission of becoming a millionaire at a young age. Banking instruments are supposed to be tools you can use to achieve your goals; that is why you should work with a bank and products that put your interest first.

*Chapter 4*

# Budgeting Basics – The Real Secret to Managing Your Wealth

BUDGET CONTROL

I can imagine many teenagers reading this topic and wondering if it's essential or perhaps thinking, "why can't we just skip this?" I would have loved to do that, but I will not be helping you because herein lies one of the biggest secrets to becoming rich and growing richer. Also, because I know personal finance is not one of the topics taught in your classrooms.

If you are serious about being financially successful, you need to learn budgeting skills and practice them. I will also be chipping in tips from teens like you who are already applying this strategy to their lives and making millions of dollars.

Here are some tips on budgeting specifically for pre-teens and teenagers to help you start growing your newly found wealth.

## Understand Your Earnings

What is your income? Knowing what makes up your income is the first step to budgeting. If you are on the job, your income is the amount your employee pays into your account after deducting tax and other requirements. If you have extra income from other sources, that will also be added to the amount to form your total income. In a situation where your income varies every month, then it's best to play safe and work with a lesser figure.

## Break it Down

Next is to divide your budget into categories. Some of the two main categories you can find include savings and expenses. Other subcategories can later come under these two, where you can list out everything and everywhere your money will be going. Here's an example for better understanding.

**Savings:** What are the things you plan on saving towards?

- Savings Account/Investment
- College Fund
- Big Purchase like PlayStation, Laptop, or a Car
- Retirement Account

**Expenses:** What do you plan on spending your money on? This could have sub-categories and should be arranged in order of importance.

- **Necessities**
    - Phone Bill
    - Lunch Money
    - Gas Expenses
    - Medical Expenses
    - Transportations
- **Other types of expenses**
    - Games and other subscriptions
    - Gym Membership
    - Weekend/Night out/Treats (Coffee, pleasure food, ice cream, and others)
    - Entertainment and other fun activities
    - Beauty treatments

I have excluded some items like rent because most teens still live with their parents or guardians. However, if you pay a portion of the rent, that will go under the "necessary expenses category."

## Select a Budgeting Strategy

When you are done with the categories, the next thing is to decide how much goes to each one. To do this effectively, you can choose different budgeting types that best suit your situation. I have listed and explained three of them below here:

Pay Yourself First

This method suggests that the first item to get funding is your savings. For example, immediately your earnings are available, a certain percentage goes right into your savings account, and you can distribute what is left to other categories.

Zero-based Budgeting

This budgeting method is used to account for every dime you are spending to the last $0. It suggests that you should arrive at zero after you have allocated funds for all your expenses. That means you can account for every penny of your money. So, with Zero-based budgeting, you will be using an estimate or previous cost to prepare the budget for the next period. The estimate is a guide that is close to the real thing.

## The 50/30/20 Rule

This method breaks your budget into three basic categories and allocates a percentage to each:

- 50% for necessities
- 30% for other expenses
- 20% for savings

You can always alter these allocations based on your goals per time. For instance, if you are saving towards a big purchase, you can increase the allocation for your savings to 30%. Also, if your expenses are not that high, you may increase your savings.

## Save Now and Spend Later

This budgeting tip refers to the process of spending your earnings. When you get paid, save the money first, then sit down and plan your spending. If you can ask for a bank or money app payment instead of a cash payment, that will be great. That way, the money goes into your bank account and sits for some time.

On the other hand, if you receive your income and start spending before you save, there are high chances that you will either end up not saving anything or save way less than expected. When you practice the act of saving first before anything, you are boosting your chances of staying richer for a long time to come.

## Set a Goal-Oriented Budget

Budgeting is a lot of fun and easier to follow when it's target-focused. For example, if you are planning on getting a MacBook or even a car. Sometimes, it could even be to take a trip with friends. The point is, your budgeting is focused on achieving something. If you follow that budget you have drawn up, gradually, you will begin to see your dreams come through because your savings will improve, and a better spending habit will emerge.

## Spending Adjustment

One of the best benefits of using a budget is that it helps you adjust your spending habits. Your records will show you where you spend your money the most; then, you can decide how to cut down and save more where you feel the cost is high.

For example, if you enjoy stopping by a chocolate shop every now and then, you may not have bothered to keep track of how much you spend on your favorite brand. If you keep a budget, it will show you how much you spend; you can now decide if it's worth continuing with that habit or look for an alternative option so you can save a little more.

You will be surprised at how much a slight adjustment in habit can affect your saving goals.

## Adjust Your Budget

The beauty of a budget is that it can be adjusted. If you discover you are always spending more on necessities like food or gas, you can adjust that item by increasing the funds allocated. We don't want you starving in the name of saving for the future. On the other hand, if you get another job closer to your home, which means you will spend less on gas or transportation, you can allocate the extra fund to other areas or save the extra.

Another way to approach the adjustment is if you find out your budget for items under "wants" is high, you can look for cheaper ways to achieve these wants. Alternatively, you can rework your calculations for non-essentials so you can release more funds to meet these wants.

The essence of a budget is not to stifle or deprive you of having fun but to give you more control over spending your money.

## Learn from Your Mistakes

Like in every area of life, mistakes are inevitable; the lessons you learn from these mistakes matter in the end. For example, if you fall short on your savings target for a few months, you will need to skip some fun activities or settle for the least expensive options so you can catch up on your savings goals. Think about why you fell short and plan to stay on target going forward.

Financial responsibility comes from practice. So, the next time you fall short on a budget item like savings, think of better ways to improve.

## Earn More with Side Gigs

If your budget shows that there's more room for more income to come in so you can achieve your dreams earlier, then you can try out some side gigs if you have the time and skill. We have previously listed many hustles you can do to make more money.

When it comes to time, teenagers have a tremendous advantage over adults. So, make the most of the time in your hand and push in some cash into your savings and investment accounts.

## Spend Moderately

When it comes to anything "spending," the lesser, the better. When your earning comes in or when you get paid, spend as sparingly as possible. Here are some suggestions that can help:

- Check out some top quality second-hand items as against the new ones
- Consider appreciating what you already have instead of spending extra on new ones that perform the same functions

- For clothing, try out a capsule wardrobe and only spend on selected, high-quality clothes

## Avoid Peer Pressure

Nothing derails a teenager's budget like peer pressure. From keeping up with the latest trends in fashion to paying for everyone when you stop for a bite with friends, you are more likely to be tempted to spend outside your budget. You need to pick a side a lot of the time to stay focused on achieving your dream. Alternatively, you offer them home-cooked meals instead of hanging out at expensive food places that will hurt your pocket. A real friend will not mind what you're wearing to hang out with them and will not mind your choice of location for a meal or fun.

Life as a teen comes with many pressures. Whether it's keeping up with current fashion trends or grabbing a bite to eat with friends, you may be tempted to overspend often. Don't feel bad about not having the latest accessories or asking your friends to hang out instead of dining out at the park. True friends are happy to hang out with you regardless of what you're wearing or where you are.

## Ask for Help

Remember to ask for help when working on your budget. Ask your parents, guardians, and even financial experts for help when you get stuck. You will be amazed how their wealth of experience can help move your dreams up. You can also follow other teens who are doing well and better financially on social media. Podcasts and books are also other ways of understanding the minds of the writers or speakers.

## Balance Your Budget

Balancing your budget means you have to ensure your spending does not exceed your income. If, by chance, your expenses exceed your available income, then you will have a negative budget. That means you're spending more money than you are earning. In that case, you will need to revisit the items on your budget and look for items to make more cuts.

## Please, Have Fun

You will notice how I have mentioned this many times in this book. Have fun! As teenagers, you have the advantage of having these items in better ways than your parents and other adults. Technology and social media have made budgeting a lot more fun than it used to be. Right from your App Store or Google Play Store, you will find loads of apps that will make budgeting easier for you. You will be able to track your spending live in real-time.

Before you start considering the idea of cruising through without a budget, let me quickly show you how operating without a budget can derail your financial success.

## Negative Implications of not Having a Budget

There are several negative implications of not working with a budget, and the longer it takes you to implement a budget, the further you will move away from your dreams. Also, you will lose absolute control over your finances because you can't track how you're spending.

Consider these adverse consequences and see if this is what you want for your finances.

- Difficulty in achieving your financial dreams: If you want to achieve your dreams of being richer soon, you need to start using a budget to tell you how you spend, your progress, and the areas where you need to make adjustments. The lack of budgeting means you are "driving blind." You don't know where you're going or how to get there. For example, if you need to buy a PlayStation console for $500, a budget will show you how much you need to save monthly to achieve that based on your income. It will further tell you if you need to achieve the goal faster and what you need to do, but without a budget, $500 might remain in your dreams and look impossible to achieve.

- Inconsistent Savings. When you don't know your actual income and monthly expenses, you will certainly not know how much to put away for savings. A budget is a breakdown of everything and where your money goes. With a budget, you will be more consistent with your saving habits.

- You will have less financial control. Everyone that wants to be financially successful must be in control of their finances. That's the kind of power a budget gives you; you get to call the shots rather than your money controlling you or living on impulse.

- When you don't use a budget, you will find it easy to overspend. Budgeting creates limits, and if you stay within those limits, you will be fine. However, when you don't have a budget, there are no limits at all, and you will go further and further away from your goals, and if you don't watch it, you might end up in enormous debts.

- Being in debt is not the issue, but knowing how to get out of it is the most critical challenge. When you operate your expenses with a budget guide, you will know how to pay your debts. However, the absence of a budget will drive you deeper into debts, and you can start to kiss your financial success goodbye.

- When you are living your life without a budget, it becomes more challenging to make bigger purchases. It's even more challenging to meet unexpected or sudden expenses because you have failed to prepare for the rainy day.

- The lack of a budget makes you lack financial contentment. When you live without a budget, it makes you live and spend money at will. It will not matter if what you are spending money on is a need or a want; you keep spending until you run out of cash.

- The most challenging part of not having a budget is the stress that comes with it. The feeling of not being in control of your finances can be stressful. The fact that you know you're spending above your means but lack the will to control it can also weigh on your mind.

Isn't it just better to get a budget today and prevent all these negative implications? It's easier to work with a budget that deals with all these consequences.

## Debts Will Kill Your Dreams of Becoming Rich

As a teenager, if you learn how to be financially responsible from a young age by learning how money works and how to manage your money yourself, you will enjoy a higher standard of living. Additionally, you will not have to run to your parents and guardians all the time for financial bailouts. Did I mention that you will also be financially independent?

The advantage of being financially responsible is endless. For example, you will know how to avoid debts by avoiding excessive student loans, credit card debts, and car loan payments. These are some of the items that can hold you down for a long time and prevent you from rising to that financial height you have been working hard to achieve.

Let's discuss this topic a little further.

## Your Freedom Depends on Your Level of Debt

When you are indebted to someone, you become their slave. It's the same as being in handcuffs because you will never be free until you're done paying off that debt. Teenagers are mostly the ones that fall for all these ridiculous offers from financial institutions. They end up accepting too many "deals" like Zero-down Financing, No Payments for 12 months, No Limits on Spending, and other tricks used to attract young people by banks, home improvement retailers, furniture stores, and car dealerships.

According to a study by TransUnion, in the U.S., 66% of Gen Z consumers age 18 and above have credit card loans, bank loans, or mortgages. Among the 66% of young people who are "credit active," half of them have a credit card. The danger is that credit most often leads to uncontrolled spending, impulse buying, and unnecessary purchases of expensive items, all of which defeats the idea of using the credit card to build a credit score. Credit cards always lead to debts if you are not disciplined because you will pay the actual cost of the item and still pay the bank interest and penalty if you are late.

So, stay focused on the cash-flow effect of a big purchase and avoid recurring financial commitments by all means.

## Back Off from Credit Card Debts

As much as possible, avoid credit card debts. Let me show why I have been emphasizing this matter. If you are paying 20% interest on your credit card, that brings you to negative payments.

When you're indebted, you will find it difficult to invest because most of your resources will go towards servicing debts, which can go on for a long time. Other types of debts that teenagers fall into include student loans and car leases, among others.

## Invest in Your Retirement Today

As a teenager, the day you become eligible to open a retirement account is the best time to start investing in your future. The longer you delay, the more challenging it becomes to achieve a reasonable retirement. For example, if you delay till you're 40 before you start investing $20,000 every year, you will only end up with half the investment a 21-year-old would have invested if they started investing $5,000 per year. When you start investing early, even the smallest amount can turn into good fortune.

## Choose Your School Wisely

Everyone wants to attend the best schools, and as we know, education is no longer cheap. So, sometimes because we want to attend some schools, we are willing to go into debts that will take a long time to pay off.

What's the fun in attending a $50,000 university and ending up with a student loan for many years when you could have opted for an affordable alternative? After all, what you do with the degree is what matters in the end and not the institution's name on the degree.

Carrying the burden of a student loan can stand in the way of your becoming rich for a long time because just a few months after graduation, you will be expected to start making payments. The loan pressure can cloud your judgment and lead to you doing jobs below your qualification because you need to meet the loan payments. That is how it starts and goes on till you lose control of your finances.

## Little Expenses Lead to Big Problems

There's an unconscious way teenagers land into debt that you need to pay attention to and avoid. For example, if you want to buy a laptop that costs $300, you will most likely check more than three sellers for the best price. You can even go further by checking for discounts and all that. Isn't that right?

However, without even giving it a thought, you will spend $60 at a restaurant, $30 at the movies, $40 for that special belt that just hit the market, $25 on coffee, and a few other "small" expenses here and there.

These expenses look okay at first glance, but they start to add up and eat deeper into your pocket over time. Unconsciously, you will not know when you have incurred thousands in expenses. On the flip side, by taking care of these little foxes and consciously putting $3 here and $5 extra in your investment account, you can comfortably retire when you're ready.

According to a recent study by Mint Survey, younger adults are the least likely to know how much they spend, with only 23% of respondents between age 18 and 24 claiming they knew how much they spent in the previous months, compared to 27% of Millennials, 34% of Gen X and 46% of Baby Boomers.

Whether you have a lot of money or are in a tight financial situation, you need a budget. A simple monthly budget will help you track your spending, improve your financial responsibilities and achieve your set goals.

If you are serious about being rich and getting a car, buying a house soon, and getting all the good things in life, like a good investment that keeps growing, then having and using a budget is critical to achieving all these.

*Chapter 5*

# Investment – Growing and Multiplying Your Wealth

As a teenager, you have everything going for you when it comes to time and investment. The earlier you start, the quicker you begin to see the result of your investment yielding good returns. Time also gives you the advantage of a quick recovery when something goes wrong. For example, if the market goes against your projections, you have time to recover and do better. Also, if the market goes south because you are young, you have the patience to wait for a recovery.

Not only do you have time for your funds to grow and for you to recover from a bad movement against your investment, but you can also start benefiting from youth tax breaks.

Another benefit of starting early as a teenager or someone younger is that you will start learning essential investment lessons as you gain experience, all of which will be useful to you as you grow older. However, I must admit that knowing where to start as a teenager is a bit challenging. For the most part, you will need the guidance of an adult or an expert to help you set up and manage the account until you get to the legal age permitted.

Below are a few ways to invest as a teenager, the types of investment you can access at your age, and the best options for you.

## When Can You Start Investing?

While it is true that there are several apps that you can easily download and sign up for on your phone, you should be aware of your country's rules on investing by minors before funding any of these free investment apps. In most countries, the law requires you to be at least 18 years old.

As a minor, you're not allowed to invest in the stock market by yourself, especially under 18 years. There are investment apps like Webull and Robinhood that seem perfect for investments by teenagers to start trading on their own. The point is that legally, you are still not allowed to participate in the stock market on your own.

There is a way out for you as a teenager or minor to invest in the stock market, and that is through a custodial account. This is your best approach to investing in the stock market until you come of age.

## What's a Custodial Account?

A custodial account is a type of financial investment account maintained by an adult, like a parent or guardian, on behalf of another person who is usually a minor. A custodial account can be an investment account or a standard savings account, and they are usually held at a brokerage, bank, or any other financial institution.

There are basically two types of custodial accounts;

- The Uniform Transfer Minors Act Account (UTMA)
- Uniform Gifts to Minors Act Account (UGMA)

If you are a teenager interested in starting on investment instead of waiting till you are 18 or more, you can talk to your parents or guardian about setting up this type of account on your behalf.

The UTMA can be set up with a wide range of different types of investment accounts. The fund in this investment account will be controlled by your custodian, who can be your parents or guardians. You will not have any form of control until your 18<sup>th</sup> birthday. I think it's important to mention that the legal age could be 21 years for some states or countries.

The UGMA type of account allows your investment to be managed and controlled in your custodian's name in your interest without your custodian necessarily setting up a special trust on your behalf. However, UGMA is mainly held in the Minor's name, which means the money belongs to you, but your listed trustee can carry out transactions on your behalf until you attain the legal age when you can now take over the account and the investment.

When you come of age and have access to this account, you can use it for any purpose you desire. However, there will be certain investment income limits. That means that the issue of taxation starts to come, which will be based on your child's tax rate. The child tax rate is calculated based on age and your status as a student or not.

For better understanding, if you are below 19 years (whether you're a student or not) or younger than 24 years, but you are a full-time student. In this scenario, your first #1,100 of income from either of these investment accounts will not be taxed, but your next $1,100 will be taxed at 10%. Everything after that will be taxed at your parents' marginal tax rates called "Kiddie Tax."

## How to Invest as a Teen

Diversification remains a robust approach when planning investment, and it doesn't matter what age you are. It simply means "not putting all your eggs in one basket." So, as a teenager, your best investment approach will be a combination of stocks, mutual funds, and exchange-traded funds (ETFs). Stocks have been described as the most exciting investment vehicle, but they are also the riskiest.

Before committing funds to purchase any stock, make sure you do extensive research on the stock and the stock market. If you need to take an investment class, please do it. Also, before you start trading, create a virtual demo trading account where you can practice how to trade and all these other things you learned in your investment class. After you have practiced for some months, practice some more and when you're ready to invest real money, start with the least amount you can afford.

There's a general warning that comes with most traded instruments where they warn you to only trade with funds you are willing to lose.

### Investment in Individual Stocks

Investing in individual stocks could lead to a better chance of faster capital appreciation because they tend to appreciate quicker and outpace a broader collection of stocks in multiple companies. On the other hand, you could be exposed to a greater level of risk because you're putting all your eggs in one basket. Investment in individual stock will expose you to the ups and downs of a single company with no cushion to absorb the risk.

The focus of growth stock is more long-term in capital appreciation and not about paying dividends to the investors. As you start your investment journey, you will get to a point where you have to decide whether to invest for capital appreciation or dividends.

As a teen, if you choose to invest in dividend-yielding stocks, it can grow into something lucrative in the long run. Dividends are a share of the profit paid to investors by the company. The amount you will get as a dividend will depend on the number of shares of the company you hold.

Under normal circumstances, healthy companies see their stock price appreciate every year, so if you reinvest your dividend in buying more company shares, you will start to experience gradual growth in your investment. Before you know it, it will grow into something attractive. For example, if you invested in Apple stock ten years ago, you would be worth millions today, irrespective of the quantity of your stock.

Before you start trading individual stock, consider starting with stocks for kids and take time to understand all the trading risks involved.

## Investment in Mutual Funds

Another option is to consider investing in mutual funds. This type of investment puts together funds from various investors to buy different types of investments like bonds, real estate, stocks, and others. With mutual funds, you are not in charge of trading. The fund managers do all the trading and other activities on your behalf.

Mutual funds are relatively safer than individual stocks because they involve shares of different types of companies from different sectors of the economy. Even the shares of international companies are sometimes involved in mutual fund investments. So, the risk is spread across boards, as opposed to an individual stock.

Mutual funds give you the opportunity of having an expert work for you. So, even if you are underage, you can inform your guardians or parents to help purchase some shares on your behalf in mutual funds. Your joint account also allows you to purchase other investments.

## Investment in Index Fund ETFs

Like mutual funds, ETFs provide instant diversification to investors. The significant difference includes the fact that mutual funds cost the same when you wish to buy the shares at any time of the day. On the other hand, the prices of an ETF change throughout the day. That is, the price you would have bought the shares in the morning might differ when the session is on or at the close of business. This is so because ETFs are traded on exchanges similar to stock.

Another difference is that ETFs, for the most part, do not have investment managers trading on your behalf as you have in mutual funds. This could be an advantage because the shares might be slightly lower in cost, and other expenses involved in mutual funds will be avoided when dealing with ETFs. This is particularly true for index funds because they track a broader market index, removing the need for active stock-picking.

A suggested strategy will be to invest in mutual funds and ETFs as a form of diversifying your portfolio. However, it may be more in ETFs because it provides instant diversification at a lower cost, and it doesn't try to outperform the market by taking too much risk.

Mutual fund investment managers sometimes take on an enormous risk that does not necessarily yield positive returns. Also, don't forget the other charges you must incur, irrespective of whether you made a profit or loss.

This is why ETFs are the preferred investment vehicles for teenagers because they pay off better in the long run.

Another advantage of ETFs is that your money is liquid. You can sell your position and use the money for anything you desire. Also, like stock, some ETFs pay dividends.

## Let's Talk About Micro Investing Apps

Micro investing apps are a recent trend among the younger generations, and teenagers quickly fall for it. It should be worth considering seeing that it's stress-free and fun.

These investing apps round up a fraction of every amount you spend and invest that fraction on your behalf. It's that simple. For example, if you spend $5.25 on coffee, the app might deduct an additional 75 cents from your account and invest it on your behalf.

You will have the opportunity to pre-set how you want the "round up" to be. Some prefer to round up to the nearest dollar, while others prefer to use a fraction of the percentage. Once the initial setting is done correctly, the app will do the rest. You don't even need to pay attention to it; it will keep deducting and investing for you.

The deductions are mostly irrelevant amounts, but if you add your busy card to the app, you can see your investment grow gradually over time. In no time, you would have a passive income coming in without knowing much about it.

This strategy is fast gaining ground with teenagers because it works like an advanced piggy bank or a banking app for kids. However, it does a lot more than those two because rather than your money sitting and doing nothing, the investing app is working and multiplying your money for you.

Some of these apps allow you to set flexible rules. For example, you are allowed to make a one-time deposit through the. You can also set a rule that says that a certain percentage should be deducted and invested anytime you spend at your favorite food place.

The beauty of these apps is that they are "set it and forget it." It works perfectly for teenagers because you have a lot of years ahead of you to see your investment grow.

## How to Start Investing Today

If you have some funds, you have saved up or got a big payoff from your job. I recommend you start investing today. If you do, you will have a significant financial advantage as you approach adulthood.

You can graduate from the regular piggy bank to the standard savings account. If your money is relatively significant, you can consider a custodial account or a high-yield savings account; you can begin leveraging compounding interest.

Ultimately, whichever strategy you choose, the sooner you start, the better. Take time to study the offers of the top financial services and investing apps targeted at teenagers and pre-teens to leverage the type of bank account they are offering, and the retirement investment accounts.

Let me show you something remarkable.

If your parents or guardian have been saving $1 a day from the day you were born using any of the investing apps like the Micro investment app discussed earlier, you could have earned $14,406 when you turn 18 based on an 8% average annual return.

It gets even more interesting if we assume that your parents have now given you access to this fund, and you have gone ahead and invested the same in your retirement account, which will be due when you are 68 years old. Even without contributing the $1 a day, you will end up with $776,221, based on an 8% annual return.

If you decide to continue contributing the same $1 per day until you are 68 years old at the same 8% return. Your investment could reach $1,014,168.96. By the end of the period, you would have earned a whopping $981,756 return from only $18,000 daily, $1 per day, and an initial $14,406 deposit. Imagine if you increased the daily deposit to $5 per day.

# What's All the Hype About Cryptocurrency?

Cryptocurrencies seem to have crept on everybody and have been in the spotlight for some time. Only recently, Bitcoin's market cap reached 1 trillion, NFTs sold for tens of millions, Dogecoin hit the skies in price, and Coinbase went public. So, this book will not be complete without looking at cryptocurrency, its recent price appreciation, and what's in it for you as a teenager.

A recent study by Piper Sandler revealed that, in a study of 7,000 teens from the U.S., 9% claimed they had traded cryptocurrencies. 81% of the group were male. The result further shed light on the type of cryptocurrencies the teens invested their money in and if they were buying and selling the digital currency or just holding for price appreciation.

Generally, there are no official age restrictions to being involved in any form of cryptocurrency. However, some popular ones like Coinbase, Binance, Gemini, and Kraken require you to be 18 years and above before having an account with them.

## What exactly is a cryptocurrency?

*"A cryptocurrency is a digital or virtual currency that is secured by cryptography, which makes it nearly impossible to counterfeit or double-spend. Many cryptocurrencies are decentralized networks based on blockchain technology—a distributed ledger enforced by a disparate network of computers. A defining feature of cryptocurrencies is that they are generally not issued by any central authority, rendering them theoretically immune to government interference or manipulation."* – Definition by Investopedia.

## Here's How Cryptocurrencies Work

It's essential to have at least a fair understanding of what you are putting your money into. Admittedly, cryptos are pretty confusing when you attempt to dig deeper than the surface explanation to understand what drives them and how they work. However, I will still provide you with the most straightforward understanding beyond the extensive jargon and technicalities.

Anywhere you turn these days, you can find thousands of cryptocurrencies all over the place, but one thing in common with nearly all of them is blockchain technology.

Here's a definition of blockchain that I find pretty straightforward from Euromoney,

*"Blockchain is a system of recording information in a way that makes it difficult or impossible to change, hack, or cheat the system. A blockchain is essentially a digital ledger of transactions that is duplicated and distributed across the entire network of computer systems on the blockchain. Each block in the chain contains a number of transactions, and every time a new transaction occurs on the blockchain, a record of that transaction is added to every participant's ledger. The decentralized database managed by multiple participants is known as Distributed Ledger Technology (DLT)"* – extracted from Euromoney – Blockchain Explained.

Before recent developments, cryptos were not accepted like regular currencies for everyday transactions, but all that is gradually becoming history as more big corporations embrace and accept the digital currency. Part of the reason for this slow acceptance is the unstable nature of the digital currencies because one minute, the prices are regular, and by the next, they have hit the roof.

There are a few stable currencies like Tether, which is tied to the U.S. Dollar, but the big names and big movers like Bitcoin, Ethereum, Cardano, and Polkadot have seemed to rally recklessly, throwing investors into significant gains and big losses. They have been described as depreciating and appreciating assets.

Some critics of cryptocurrencies believe that they should not have been called currencies but "crypto assets" because they are not used daily like the dollar, euro pounds, and other known currencies.

## What is the value of cryptocurrency?

As mentioned earlier, there are thousands of cryptocurrencies out there. Each has its value and tries to serve different purposes, making it challenging to have a universal value.

Here's what some experts said about the value of some of the popular cryptocurrencies;

### Bitcoin

Some have compared the value of Bitcoin, which is the world's largest cryptocurrency, with that of gold. *"As part of the transition toward a digital economy, Bitcoin could challenge gold as a global store of value. Economic history suggests that an asset accrues value as the demand for it increases relative to the supply. Demand is a function of an asset's ability to serve the three roles of money: store of value, medium of exchange, and unit of account"* – **Bitcoin as an Investment** by Yassine Elmandjra, an analyst at ARK Invest.

## Ethereum

Ethereum allows you to create "smart contracts." A smart contract is defined as a self-executing contract with the terms of the agreement between the buyer and the seller, directly written in code. *"A 'smart contract' is simply a program that runs on the Ethereum blockchain. It's a collection of code (its functions) and data (its state) that resides at a specific address on the Ethereum blockchain. User accounts can then interact with a smart contract by submitting transactions that execute a function defined on the smart contract. Smart contracts can define rules, like a regular contract, and automatically enforce them via the code"* – Extracted from ethereum.org.

This support for a smart contract has decentralized the industry further to a whole new level. Today, there are several applications of the blockchain. A good example is a decentralized finance known as "Defi," which is fast growing in the industry and encouraging the exchange of arts and collectibles through NFTs. All on the Ethereum blockchain.

## NFTs

Non-fungible tokens or NFTs represent some form of ownership of something. Several items, including collectibles, art, video games, and even real estate, can be converted into NFTs.

*"Non-fungible tokens or NFTs are cryptographic assets on blockchain with unique identification codes and metadata that distinguish them from each other. Unlike cryptocurrencies, they cannot be traded or exchanged at equivalency. This differs from fungible tokens like cryptocurrencies, which are identical to each other and, therefore, can be used as a medium for commercial transactions"* – as defined by Investopedia.

As an NFT creator, you can sell it off or charge a fixed price for it. The buyer of your NFT, too, can later sell or auction them to a different buyer. All these transactions are tracked and verified by the blockchain.

## Chainlink

This particular crypto allows the linking of real-world data to blockchains. *"Through the use of secure oracles, Chainlink extends the functionality of blockchains by connecting smart contracts to real-world data, events, payments, and more in a highly tamper-resistant and reliable manner"* – Extracted from Chainlink website.

With Chainlink, you can use real-world data on smart contracts.

## How Teens Can Invest in Cryptocurrency

To a large extent, there are no laws that prevent you from buying, selling, or investing in cryptos, but some exchanges prevent teens below the age of 18 from being directly involved. However, there are still legal ways you can be a player in the crypto space even if you are under 18.

There are several apps and methods to buy and trade Bitcoin as a teenager, but most of them are outrageously expensive and complex to use. Below are a few legal ways you can get around some of these challenges.

### Greyscale

Greyscale is a company that owns and sells multiple cryptocurrency funds that are publicly traded on the stock market, similar to mutual funds or ETFs. As a teenager interested in investing in crypto, this may be the easiest way for you. An extract from the company's website better explains what they do, *"a trusted authority on digital currency investing, Grayscale provides secure access and diversified exposure to the digital currency asset class."*

The way it works is that the company buys and stores the digital currency. Interested investors can then buy shares of their trust on the stock market floor. Your access to investing if you are under 18 is through a custodial investment account. The challenge here is that when you buy the shares of a Greyscale fund, you do not directly own a cryptocurrency; instead, you own a derivative.

That means there's a slight disparity between the crypto price and the fund's price because Greyscale funds are publicly traded, so the price is determined by the market like other stocks traded on the exchange. For better understanding, if the demand for Bitcoin drops on the exchange, the price of Greyscale's Bitcoin Trust would fall, even when the price of Bitcoin in the open market is not going down. These minor issues might make the Greyscale fund unattractive to teenagers.

## Transfer

Under this method, you still need the help of a trusted adult. The method allows you to own a cryptocurrency directly, unlike what Greyscale offers. The process is listed below;

1. The first step is to create a cryptocurrency wallet. *"Crypto wallets keep your private keys – the passwords that give you access to your cryptocurrencies – safe and accessible, allowing you to send and receive cryptocurrencies like Bitcoin and Ethereum"* – as defined by Coinbase. The wallets only support specific cryptos, and they cannot be combined, so you need to choose

which one you're interested in investing in. take time to study the best Bitcoin and Ethereum wallets available to choose from.

2. After creating the wallet, you can get a trusted adult to help you buy and fund the wallet with your desired crypto after registering with a trusted or reputable exchange.

3. Once the crypto is in your wallet, you have complete control over how you want to treat it. You may choose to hold on and watch the price appreciate (or depreciate) or use it to transact with other businesses. However, because you're not using an exchange, it may be challenging to sell your crypto.

## Peer to peer exchanges

These exchanges are marketplaces where sellers trade cryptocurrencies directly with people willing to buy from them. The way it works is that sellers can create "listings" to determine what price they are willing to part with their crypto, the payment method that works for them, and the minimum amount they can buy. While this looks good and straightforward, it comes with two main challenges:

- Outrageous Prices: Because these transactions are not happening through exchanges, the sellers charge a premium in prices. They determine the price that works for them, and the buyer has to decide too if they can afford it or not. To exchange crypto with a trusted seller, you sometimes have to pay a 10 to 20% premium.

- Prone to Scams: In addition to the outrageous prices, there is a chance that you might be dealing with people who have fraudulent intentions. This is common on P2P exchanges. Malicious sellers have been known to lure buyers with low premiums. If you must buy or sell via P2P exchanges, be sure to deal with sellers with great reviews who are well rated.

The cryptocurrency space is still evolving, and young people embrace it quicker than the generations before them. We have also seen an increase in institutional interest in this space, giving more credence that crypto has come to stay. However, I recommend that you approach this space with caution to avoid losing everything you have worked for. Speculation still drives the market up and down, and this may not be good for your investment.

## The Story of the Tampa Teen Who Made Thousands from Cryptocurrency

I would like to leave you with this story written by Jenny Dean about a Tampa teen who believes cryptocurrency is the future of finance. The story was published at www.wtsp.com. The 19-year old said he has already invested and made thousands of dollars.

*"As I've come more to understand it, I've put more and more faith into crypto, and not only do I invest in it as a financial mover, but I kind of see it as the future of finance."*

When this economics major got his stimulus check last year, he took that money and invested it in cryptocurrency. Hill quickly made a couple of thousand dollars, but he had studied it for a while before investing.

*"They have fixed inflation area or deflation area rates, and it's all very extremely transparent. There's a blockchain ledger for each of them where you can see every single transaction and how much goes to what address, etcetera."*

He thinks more people should invest, but not before doing a ton of research and at least having a basic understanding of how it works and how to store it safely.

*"I've understood it enough, I've learned about it enough where I trust it more than the U.S. dollars. And I want to pay my rent in crypto, I want to get paid in crypto, and I want to buy my groceries in crypto, and I really see that in the future."*

When this 19-year-old told his mother, a financial planner, that he wanted to put his stimulus money into cryptocurrency, she was a little skeptical. But Hill says the more she researched it, she became interested and wound up making her significant investment.

# Conclusion

As we draw the curtain on this book, I desire that this will be the beginning of a positive financial change in your life. I'm hoping that you will start putting your superpowers to good use from now. The more you use them, the better you get at mastering them, and soon you will be richer than you ever imagined. In case you are wondering what these superpowers are, I will mention a few of them again.

- The Power of Time: As a pre-teen or teenager, this is an incredible power you have at your disposal. If you start using your time better from this moment, you will be in total control of your future, especially financially.

- The Power of Savings: If you want to be rich, you must learn to start saving better from now on. The savings you start today is what will shape your future of being rich.

- The Power of Budget: If you are ever going to have a weakness as a superhero who is in control of his finances, it will come from your lack of budgeting. So, start getting it right from this moment. Set up a budget and start tracking your spending. Before you part away with your money, always remember to double-check if the item is a need or a want.

All these sound simple and maybe funny, but that's the key to you becoming rich and changing the course of your life. Don't forget to start planning for your retirement, and as mentioned before, now that you are young, you stand a better chance of retiring with some good money in your name.

Don't forget to keep your credit history clean. If you feel you cannot stay entirely out of debt, that is okay. However, make certain that you pay any debts owed to banks or the government on or before the due date. That way, you will keep your credit history clean and healthy.

Now is not the time to start bothering too much about mistakes. I can assure you, you will make mistakes just as those teen millionaires too did, but you have the time to learn from these mistakes and get better. It is called "failing forward." If you have the right mindset backed by a great attitude, failure will not keep you down but rather push you to do better.

I will repeat it one more time, don't lose yourself in the process of becoming the wealthiest young person around. Take time to have fun. Having fun doesn't mean being extravagant. There are cost-effective ways of having fun and still staying on track to becoming a wealthy teenager.

## Follow the Right Influencers

Social media is here to stay, and teenagers are glued to it like a magnet. Well, if you're going to spend a lot of time on social media checking out your influencers, why not start following the suitable influencers who speak your language? I mean the millionaire language, and they are young people like you, some even younger. It's a great way to level up your mindset.

Here's a list of people you can start following right away, all from TikTok.

## Humphrey Yang

**Handle: @humphreytalks | 2.3M followers**

Check him out for tips on credit cards, passive income, and easy investing strategies.

Humphrey Yang is a former financial advisor turned entrepreneur and social media star. He shares personal finance and entrepreneurship tips with his 2.3 million TikTok followers and 224K YouTube subscribers.

## Tori Dunlap

**Handle: @Herfirst100k | 1.7M followers**

Tori Dunlap's videos focus on helping others grow their money. As her handle suggests, she encourages others to save and reach the goal of their first $100,000 in savings. Tori also advocates for fair salaries for women and offers tips on handling salary negotiations in a firm but professional manner.

## Steve Financial Freedom Coach

### Handle: @calltoleap | 848K followers

As a former public school teacher who worked hard for financial freedom, Steve posts personal finance videos on TikTok, playing out different money scenarios to help empower others in those same situations. Watch Steve for his credit card hacks and passive income ideas.

## Ellyce Fullmore

### Handle: @millennial_coach | 357.2K followers

As a self-proclaimed "money coach," Ellyce Fullmore offers personal finance tips aimed at a Millennial and Gen Z audience. She keeps things fun by lip-syncing and dancing to popular music while explaining financial terms through text. She also regularly answers financial questions submitted by her viewers.

## Coach Vince

### Handle: @thedollerman | 144K followers

Coach Vince posts short videos discussing investing for beginners and financial freedom. Vince likes to break down investing concepts like risk and reward, and he often advises on staying calm when the market is in decline. Ask Vince a question about investing, and you might be featured on one of his TikTok.

You have been equipped to go out there and conquer all fears and limiting beliefs. Start making money today and watch it grow into millions in a short while. Start rewriting your financial future from this moment on.

Also, if you enjoyed this book, don't keep the secret to yourself. Would you please share it with your friends? It's more fun when you are all millionaires together. Don't forget to leave us an excellent review on the platform where you purchased the book. Your review will go a long way in helping other people worldwide enjoy the secrets exposed in this book.

# A Plea From the Author

I hope you enjoyed the book and found it informative and useful. I will very much appreciate if you can leave a review on Amazon to show your satisfaction and support the author.

You can log into your Amazon account or go to:
amazon.com/ryp

# References

Esan, I.M (December 2020) 5 Common Mistakes Teenagers Make with Money. Teens Meet Online.
https://teensmeetonline.com/2020/12/24/common-teenagers-money-mistakes/

Five Tips for Teens to Avoid Debt. Boys and Girls Club of America
https://www.bgca.org/news-stories/2019/November/Five-tips-for-teens-to-avoid-debt

8 Painful Consequences of Not Budgeting. Be The Budget
https://bethebudget.com/consequences-of-not-budgeting/

Jenny, D. (2021). Tampa Teen Believes Cryptocurrency is the Future of Finance. Tampa Bay.
https://www.wtsp.com/article/money/teens-and-cryptocurrency/67-72654d15-dd81-4e2d-894c-c2e4e4866399

Eli, (April 2021). A Teenagers Guide to Investing in Cryptocurrency. Teen Finance Factory.
https://teenfinancetoday.com/a-teenagers-guide-to-investing-in-cryptocurrency/

Susan, P. (September 2018). 4 Things Young People Waste Money on and How to Spend Less on Them. Saving Advice.
https://www.savingadvice.com/

articles/2018/09/05/1061224_4-things-young-people-waste-moneyon-and-how-to-spend-less-on-them.html

Arewaoba, (June 2018). 5 Things Teenagers Do Not Know About Money. Teens Meet Online
https://teensmeetonline.com/2018/06/16/5-things-teenagers-do-not-know-about-money/

Aron, M.W. Ph.D., (2003). What Happened? Alcohol, Memory Blackout, and the Brain. National Institute for Alcohol Abuse and Alcoholism.
https://pubs.niaaa.nih.gov/publications/arh27-2/186-196.htm

Crispus, N. 6 Common Teen Money Mistakes to Avoid Today. Fifi Finance.
https://fififinance.com/us/teen-money-mistakes#teen-money-mistakes-not-learning-new-skills

Kalen, B. Wanna be a Millionaire? Learn from these 12 Kids who Already Are. Like Hack.
https://www.lifehack.org/articles/money/wanna-millionaire-learn-from-these-12-kids-who-already-are.html

A 2010 Daily Mail Report on Christian Owens. Daily Mail UK.
https://www.dailymail.co.uk/news/article-1302771/amp/Christian-Owens-schoolboy-entrepreneurmaking-million-16.html

Emil Motycka - A Cool Story of a 13 Year Old Entrepreneur
https://businessideaslab.com/emil-motycka-entrepreneur/

Kate, K. (September 2020). A-Teens Guide to Banking. Step.
https://step.com/money-101/post/a-teens-guide-to-banking#paypal-venmo-cash--money-apps

Dylan, H. (May 2021). All the Best Way for Teens to Make Money (38 Ideas). Swift Salary https://www.swiftsalary.com/ways-for-teens-to-make-money/

Sarah, (September 2021). How to Make Money As A Teenager (25 Lucrative Way). Clever Girl Finance.
https://www.clevergirlfinance.com/blog/how-to-make-money-as-a-teenager/

Mint. Budgeting for Teens: 14 Tips for Growing Your Money Young. Intuit Mint Life.
https://mint.intuit.com/blog/budgeting/budgeting-for-teens/

Joshua, K. (June 2021). Teach Your Teen Financial Responsibility. The Balance.
https://www.thebalance.com/teach-your-teen-financial-responsibility-356152

Riley, A. CPA. (October 2021). How to Invest as a Teenager or a Minor (Start Under 18 Years Old). Young and the Invested.
https://youngandtheinvested.com/how-to-invest-as-teenager/

Kris, M. (July 2021). 9 Ways to Get Your Teens to Start Investing. Dough Roller.
https://www.doughroller.net/investing/best-investments-for-teens/

Emily, G. (April 2021). 9% US Teen Said They Have Traded Cryptocurrency. Business Insider.
https://markets.businessinsider.com/news/currencies/bitcoin-piper-sandler-teen-survey-cryptocurrency-investing-young-retail-btc-2021-4

www.ingramcontent.com/pod-product-compliance
Lightning Source LLC
Chambersburg PA
CBHW030304100526
44590CB00012B/509